Section 5 — Home and Environment

Section 6 — Education and Work

Section 7 — Grammar

Published by CGP

Contributors:
Simon Cook
Taissa Csáky
Heather Gregson
Gemma Hallam
Katherine Stewart
Jennifer Underwood
Gillian E Wallis
James Paul Wallis
Emma Warhurst

With thanks to Pippa Mayfield, Latefa Mansarit and Raquel Montes for the proofreading.

No corny clichés about Spanish people were harmed in the making of this book.

ISBN: 978 1 84762 290 7

Groovy website: www.cgpbooks.co.uk
Jolly bits of clipart from CorelDRAW®
Printed by Elanders Ltd, Newcastle upon Tyne.

Based on the classic CGP style created by Richard Parsons.

Numbers and Amounts

Five, four, three, two, one. We have lift-off...

Uno, dos, tres — One, two, three...

0	cero
1	uno (un), una
2	dos
3	tres
4	cuatro
5	cinco
6	seis
7	siete
8	ocho
9	nueve
10	diez

1. 11 to 15 all end in 'ce'. But 16, 17, 18 and 19 are 'ten and six', etc.

11	once
12	doce
13	trece
14	catorce
15	quince
16	dieciséis
17	diecisiete
18	dieciocho
19	diecinueve

2. All twenty-something numbers are rolled into one — "veintiuno" etc.

21	veintiuno
22	veintidós
23	veintitrés
31	treinta y uno

After 30, numbers are joined by "y" (and), but written separately — "treinta y uno" etc.

When you put "one" in front of a masculine word, "uno" drops the "o" — e.g. veintiún caballos= 21 horses, treinta y un caballos = 31 horses. ...And before a feminine word, the "o" changes to "a" — e.g. veintiuna galletas = 21 biscuits.

20	veinte	60	sesenta
30	treinta	70	setenta
40	cuarenta	80	ochenta
50	cincuenta	90	noventa

3. Most 'ten-type' numbers end in 'nta' (except 'veinte').

4. When you get to hundreds and thousands, just put ciento, doscientos, mil (etc.) before the number. A year is written like an ordinary number.

100	ciento (cien)
101	ciento uno
200	doscientos/as
500	quinientos/as
923	novecientos veintitrés
1000	mil
1,000,000	un millón

Ciento becomes "cien" unless it's followed by a number — e.g. cien pájaros = 100 birds.

mil novecientos cuarenta y siete = 1947

1000 900 40 7

First, second, third — they're a bit different...

These always end in "o" for masculine things or "a" for feminine things.

1st	primero, primera	6th	sexto/a
2nd	segundo/a	7th	séptimo/a
3rd	tercero/a	8th	octavo/a
4th	cuarto/a	9th	noveno/a
5th	quinto/a	10th	décimo/a

1st is written 1º or 1ª. 2nd is written 2º or 2ª, etc.

NB When "primero" or "tercero" appear in front of a masculine word, they always drop the "o" — "el primer baile" = the first dance.

Tome la segunda calle a la izquierda. = Take the second street on the left.

¿Cuánto? — How much?

These words for how many or how much are important.
Write each one out in different sentences — make sure you don't cheat and skip any.

Tengo todas las manzanas. = I have all the apples.

Cada plátano es amarillo. = Every/Each banana is yellow.

all the (masc. plural):	todos los	several:	varios/as
other:	otros/as	many:	muchos/as
some:	unos/as	few:	pocos/as

all the (singular): todo el / toda la

Your days are numbered — today's the 20th...

You're bound to know a bit about numbers already — which is cool. And it means you can spend more time checking that you know the rest of the page. Learn all of these words about amounts. The best way to check is to cover up the page, and then try to write them down — right now.

Times and Dates

Time — it's one of the most precious things... especially if you want to do well in your Spanish GCSE.

¿Qué hora es? — What time is it?

There are loads of ways of saying the time in English, and there are in Spanish too.

¿Qué hora es? = What time is it?

1) Something o'clock:

It's 1 o'clock:	Es la una
It's two o'clock:	Son las dos
It's 8pm:	Son las ocho de la tarde

2) Quarter to and past, half past:

(It's) quarter past two:	(Son) las dos y cuarto
(It's) half past two:	(Son) las dos y media
(It's) quarter to three:	(Son) las tres menos cuarto

3) '... past' and '... to':

(It's) twenty past seven:	(Son) las siete y veinte
(It's) twelve minutes past eight:	(Son) las ocho y doce minutos
(It's) ten to two:	(Son) las dos menos diez

4) The 24-hour clock :

20.32:	(Son) las veinte horas treinta y dos minutos
03.14:	(Son) las tres horas catorce minutos
19.55:	(Son) las diecinueve horas cincuenta y cinco minutos

You use 'el' for all the days of the week

Without these words you won't be able to understand when anything's happening.

DAYS OF THE WEEK	
Monday:	lunes
Tuesday:	martes
Wednesday:	miércoles
Thursday:	jueves
Friday:	viernes
Saturday:	sábado
Sunday:	domingo

Voy de compras los martes. = I go shopping on Tuesdays (every Tuesday).

Days of the week are all masculine. Don't put capital letters on days.

Voy el martes. = I'm going on Tuesday.

SOME USEFUL WORDS ABOUT THE WEEK	
today:	hoy
tomorrow:	mañana
yesterday:	ayer
the day after tomorrow:	pasado mañana
the day before yesterday:	anteayer
week:	la semana
weekend:	el fin de semana
on Monday:	el lunes
on Mondays:	los lunes

Hoy es mi cumpleaños. = Today is my birthday.

Tengo un examen pasado mañana. = I've got an exam the day after tomorrow.

Fui al cine ayer. = I went to the cinema yesterday.

¿Qué hora es? Time you got a watch...

Times and dates are really handy for your writing and speaking tasks to say when things happen, and they're pretty likely to crop up in the listening and reading exams too. You need to know the days of the week and things like 'tomorrow' or 'weekend'. So find the time... and get down to it.

Times and Dates

Knowing how to say dates is really useful. If you learn all this, then you'll have no problem saying when you're going on holiday, when your birthday is... that kind of thing.

Enero, febrero, marzo, abril...

Spanish month names bear a striking resemblance to the English ones — make sure you learn what's different.

January:	enero	*July:*	julio
February:	febrero	*August:*	agosto
March:	marzo	*September:*	septiembre
April:	abril	*October:*	octubre
May:	mayo	*November:*	noviembre
June:	junio	*December:*	diciembre

Months are all masculine. They don't start with capital letters.

Se va en julio. = He's leaving in July.

in March:	en marzo	*in summer:*	en (el) verano
in October:	en octubre	*in autumn:*	en (el) otoño
in spring:	en (la) primavera	*in winter:*	en (el) invierno

You say "the 3 of May" instead of "the 3rd of May"

Here's how you say the date. It could come in handy in your speaking assessment.

1) In Spanish, they don't say "the third of May" — they say "the three of May". Weird, huh.

Llego el tres de octubre. = I am coming / I arrive on the 3rd of October.

Check out page 1 for help with the numbers, and pages 10 and 11 for how to write letters.

2) And this is how you write the date in a letter:

Londres, 5 de marzo de 2009. = London, 5th March 2009.

3) And here are some other useful bits:

in the year 2000:	en el año dos mil
in 2001:	en (el) dos mil uno

NOT 'dos mil y uno'

Mañana — Tomorrow... Ayer — Yesterday

Use these with the stuff on page 2 — great for sorting out your social life.

Voy a esquiar a menudo. = I often go skiing.

always:	siempre	*seldom:*	pocas veces
often:	a menudo	*sometimes:*	a veces

tomorrow:	mañana
yesterday:	ayer
this morning:	esta mañana
this afternoon/evening:	esta tarde
tonight:	esta noche
tomorrow morning:	mañana por la mañana
this week:	esta semana
next week:	la semana que viene
last week:	la semana pasada
every fortnight:	cada quince días
every day:	todos los días
at the weekend:	el fin de semana

See page 105 for how to say you never do something.

¿Qué haces esta noche? = What are you doing tonight?

Dates are nice if they're stuffed with marzipan...

It doesn't come much more crucial than this. Throwing a few time expressions into your speaking and writing tasks will get you more marks. It's not that hard, either. Just learn a few phrases like '¿Qué haces esta noche?', and the different words you can slot into them.

Asking Questions

You'll have to ask questions if you want to score top marks in your speaking tasks. And before you ask, "What's the Spanish for hello?" won't cut it.

1) Make it a question with ¿ ? or tone of voice

To turn a statement into a question, just add an upside down question mark to the beginning and a normal question mark to the end of the sentence. When you're speaking, raise your voice at the end to show it's a question. Peasy.

¿Tus pantalones son negros? = Are your trousers black?

(Literally: Your trousers are black?)

See the grammar section for more on endings.

¿Tienes un coche? = Do you have a car?

(Literally: You have a car?)

2) 'What' questions — stick '¿Qué' at the start

If your question starts with "What...", use "¿Qué...".

¿Qué comes por la mañana? = What do you eat in the morning?

¿Qué quieres hacer? = What do you want to do?

3) ¿Cuándo? – When? ¿Por qué? – Why? ¿Dónde? – Where?

There are loads of other question words you can slot into a sentence at the start instead of 'qué'. Look at these question words — then cover 'em up and learn 'em.

when?:	¿cuándo?
why?:	¿por qué?
where?:	¿dónde?
how?:	¿cómo?
how much?:	¿cuánto?
how many?:	¿cuántos/as?
at what time...?	¿a qué hora?
who?:	¿quién?
which...?:	¿cuál?
what?:	¿qué?
is...?:	¿es...?

¿Cuándo vuelves a casa? = When are you coming home?

¿Quién rompió la ventana? = Who broke the window?

¿Cuánto dinero tienes? = How much money do you have?

I can't read this — it's upside down...

This page is full of question words — start by learning them all. Shut the book and write down all the question words. Look back for the ones you missed and try again till you get them all.

Being Polite

You'll lose marks (and sound rude) if you don't stay polite in your speaking assessment — it's dead important.

Por favor — Please... Gracias — Thank you

Easy stuff — maybe the first Spanish words you ever learnt. Don't ever forget them.

por favor = please

gracias = thank you

thank you very much: muchas gracias

Es muy amable = That's very nice of you *(formal)*

If you're talking to a friend: Eres muy amable

de nada = you're welcome

Lo siento = I'm sorry

I'm really sorry: lo siento mucho

Excuse me! (e.g. wanting to ask the way, or attract attention):	Por favor / Perdone señor(a)
Excuse me! (e.g. wanting to get past someone):	Con permiso

Quisiera — I would like

As my mum always says, "I want never gets". It's the same in Spanish — it's much more polite to say 'quisiera' (I would like) than 'quiero' (I want).

Here's how to say you would like a thing:

Quisiera un zumo de naranja. = I would like an orange juice.

Here's how to say you would like to do something:

Quisiera hablar. = I would like to talk.

¿Puedo sentarme? = May I sit down?

go to the toilet:	ir al baño
have something to drink:	beber algo

Sorry's not the hardest word in Spanish...

These little beauties are just the ticket for excelling as a social butterfly in Spain... oh yes, and they'll help masses when it comes to your speaking tasks. These charmers are absolutely vital.

Being Polite

You'd like a page on handy meeting and greeting phrases? Your wish is my command.
The thing about Spanish is if you can say stuff politely, you're bound to pick up good marks.

¡Buenos días! ¿Qué tal? — Hello! How are you?

Good day:	Buenos días
Good evening:	Buenas tardes
How are you? (informal):	¿Qué tal?
How are you? (formal):	¿Cómo está?
Good day (to a man):	Buenos días, señor
Good day (to a woman):	Buenos días, señora/señorita
Hello:	Hola
Goodbye:	Hasta luego / Adiós

To reply to 'Buenos días', just say 'Buenos días' back. Do the same with 'Buenas tardes'.

Bien, gracias. = (I am) fine thanks.

Very well:	muy bien	*Great:*	maravillosamente bien
Not good:	no muy bien	*OK:*	bien
Not bad:	así así	*Terrible:*	fatal

See page 22 if you're not well and you need to explain why.

Le presento a Nuria — May I introduce Nuria?

My life's such a social whirl — parties, introductions... oh, have we met before...

Esta es María = This is María

For a man: Este es ...

Encantado = Pleased to meet you

If you're a girl: Encantada

Mucho gusto = Pleased to meet you

Pasa. Siéntate. = Come in. Sit down. *(Informal, singular)*

Pase. Siéntese. = Come in. Sit down. *(Formal, singular)*

Pasen. Siéntense. = Come in. Sit down. *(Formal, plural)*

Pasad. Sentaos. = Come in. Sit down. *(Informal, plural)*

You say adiós and I say hola...

It's a bit boring, I know. But grin, bear it, and most of all learn it, and you'll be fine. It'll be worth it when you show off your excellent manners in your speaking assessment. It's worth the effort.

Opinions

It pays to have an opinion, in more ways than one. Learn how to say what you think, or stay dull.

¿Qué piensas de...? — What do you think of...?

All these nifty phrases mean the same thing — 'What do you think of ...?'. Look out for them.
If you can use all of them, then your Spanish will be wildly fascinating — and that means more marks.

FINDING OUT SOMEONE'S OPINION

What do you think?:	¿Qué piensas?
What do you think of...?:	¿Qué piensas de...? / ¿Qué te parece...?
What's your opinion of...?:	¿Cuál es tu opinión de...?
Do you find him/her nice?:	¿Le encuentras simpático/a?
	¿Te parece simpático/a?

AGREEING AND DISAGREEING

I agree:	Estoy de acuerdo
I disagree:	No estoy de acuerdo
That's true:	Es verdad
That's not true:	No es verdad

¿Qué piensas de mi novio? = What do you think of my boyfriend?

Creo que está loco. = I think he's mad.

Juan me parece muy simpático. = I think Juan's very nice.

I THINK...

I think that ... :	Pienso que ...
	Creo que ...
I think ... is ... :	... me parece ...

Say what you think — it's impressive

Being able to say you like or dislike something is a good start,
but make the effort to learn something a bit more expressive too.

Me gusta el tenis de mesa, pero no me gusta el fútbol.

= I like table tennis, but I don't like football.

LIKING THINGS

I like... :	Me gusta (singular)...
	Me gustan (plural)...
I like... a lot:	Me gusta(n) mucho...
I love:	Me encanta(n)...
I'm interested in... :	Me interesa(n)...
I find... great:	Encuentro ... fantástico

When you like more than one thing, remember to add the "n".

DISLIKING THINGS

I don't like... :	No me gusta...(singular)/
	No me gustan...(plural)
I don't like at all... :	No me gusta nada...(singular)/
	No me gustan nada...(plural)
...doesn't interest me:	... no me interesa
I find ... awful:	Encuentro ... horrible/muy mal

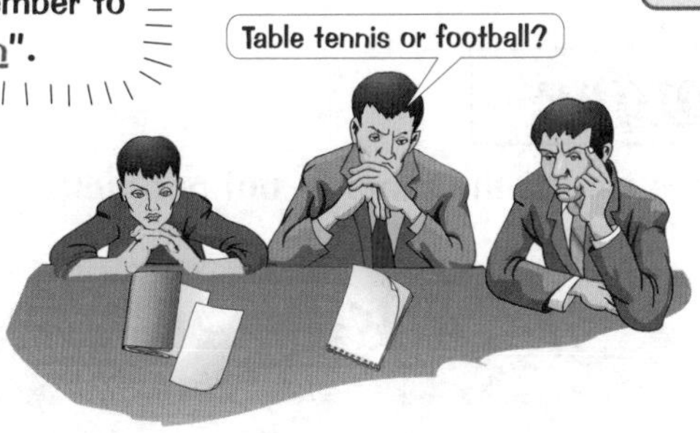

OTHER USEFUL PHRASES

It's all right:	Vale
I don't mind/care:	Me da igual
I prefer... :	Prefiero...
It's fine:	Está bien

An opinion — a prickly onion...

Never underestimate the power of opinions. It might seem hard to believe, but they really do want you to say what you think. Make sure you learn one way to say 'I like' and 'I don't like' first. They're the absolute basics — you'll get nowhere without them. Then add all the fancy bits.

Opinions

Don't just say that you like or hate something. Really go to town by explaining why you think the way you do — you're sure to pick up marks if you use some of these handy descriptions.

Use words like 'bueno' (good) to describe things

Here are a juicy bunch of words to describe things you like or don't like. They're rather easy to use, so it really is worth learning them.

good:	bueno/a	*perfect:*	perfecto/a	*nice (person):*	simpático/a
great:	estupendo/a	*fantastic:*	fantástico/a	*nice / kind:*	agradable
great:	fenomenal	*brilliant:*	magnífico/a	*marvellous:*	maravilloso/a
great:	genial	*fabulous:*	fabuloso/a	*bad:*	malo/a
beautiful:	precioso/a	*incredible:*	increíble	*awful:*	horrible
friendly:	amable	*interesting:*	interesante	*ridiculous:*	ridículo/a
excellent:	excelente	*entertaining:*	entretenido/a	*strange:*	raro/a

Owen es estupendo.

= Owen is great.

Los niños son horribles.

= The children are awful.

To say 'because' say 'porque'

Congratulations — you have an opinion, so you're officially not dull. But to reach the coveted rating of 'interesting', you need to know how to back it up with 'porque'.

'porque' is ultra-important — forget it at your peril.

Me gusta esta película porque los actores son muy buenos.

= I like this film because the actors are very good.

Pienso que esta película es horrible porque la historia es aburrida.

= I think this film is awful because the story is boring.

Don't mix up 'por qué', and 'porque'

Be careful not to mix up "why" and "because". They're almost the same — but not quite:

WHY? = ¿POR QUÉ?

BECAUSE = PORQUE

Poor Kaye? What's wrong with her...

It's not much cop only knowing how to ask someone else's opinion, or how to say 'I think', without being able to say what you think and why. All these phrases are easy — just stick them together to get a sentence. Just make sure you don't say something daft like 'I like it because it's awful'.

What Do You Think of...?

Giving opinions is one of those things that will definitely get you marks in the exam.
Learn these general phrases and you'll be able to give your opinions on a zillion different topics.

Use 'Creo que...' or 'Pienso que...' to give your opinion

¿Qué piensas de este grupo? = What do you think of this band?

Creo que este grupo es bueno. = I think this band is good.

this team:	este equipo
this magazine:	esta revista
this music:	esta música
this novel:	esta novela
this actor:	este actor
this actress:	esta actriz
this film:	esta película
this newspaper:	este periódico

bad:	malo/a
excellent:	excelente
boring:	aburrido/a
quite good:	bastante bueno/a
fantastic:	fantástico/a

You can use any of the opinion words from p. 8.

Use 'estoy de acuerdo' to agree

No me gusta este libro. Creo que es aburrido. ¿Estás de acuerdo?

These are linked. If the thing you're talking about is masculine, then the description has to be masculine too.

= I don't like this book. I think it's boring. Do you agree?

Estoy de acuerdo. = I agree.

No, no estoy de acuerdo. A mí me encanta este libro.

= No, I don't agree. I love this book.

You can also use '¿Y tú?' after giving your opinion to find out what the other person thinks.

Creo que esta película es ridícula. ¿Y tú?

= I think this film is ridiculous. How about you?

Let's just agree to disagree...

Giving your opinion about things gets you big marks in the exams. It's all a matter of having the vocab at your fingertips, ready to use. And the best way to have that is, yep, lots of practice.

Writing Informal Letters

You might need to write a letter to a friend or pen pal for one of your Spanish writing tasks.
Just remember the secret of writing a good letter in any language is knowing the rules.

Learn this layout for starting and finishing

Here's an incredibly short letter — it shows all the key bits you need for letter-writing.

Millom, 5 de marzo
Querido Juan:
¿Qué tal?
Gracias por tu carta.
Me alegró mucho recibir tus noticias.
Yo estoy muy bien.
Espero poder visitarte en Madrid en el verano.
Escríbeme pronto.
Saludos,
Albert

Put where you live and the date up here. Check out page 3 for dates.

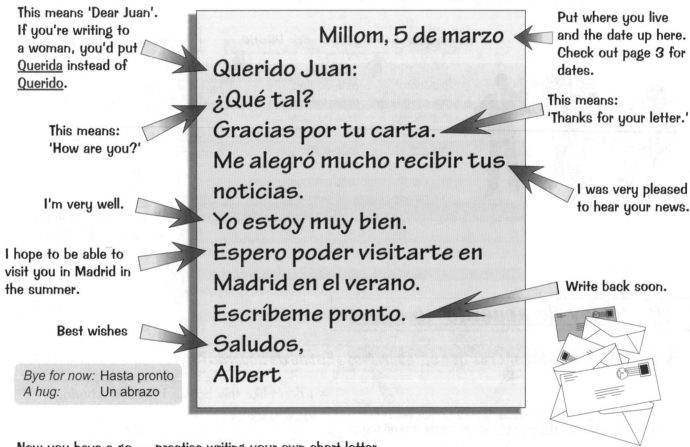

This means 'Dear Juan'. If you're writing to a woman, you'd put Querida instead of Querido.

This means: 'How are you?'

This means: 'Thanks for your letter.'

I was very pleased to hear your news.

I'm very well.

I hope to be able to visit you in Madrid in the summer.

Write back soon.

Best wishes

Bye for now: Hasta pronto
A hug: Un abrazo

Now you have a go — practise writing your own short letter.

Use plenty of common phrases in your letters

Learning the layout is all very well, but it's only the start. Writing good letters means using lots of nice clear Spanish phrases and vocab. They don't need to be complicated — just right.

¿Qué tal? = How are you?

¿Qué piensas de...? = What do you think of...?

¿Cómo va todo? = How's it all going?

This one's quite good for signing off. *Espero recibir tus noticias pronto.* = I hope to hear from you soon.

Informal letters — they keep you informed...

Think you've got it sussed — then cover up the page and practise writing a few short letters — it's the only way to make sure. Use plenty of nice simple phrases — and get 'em right.

Writing Formal Letters

Sigh... Formal letters are sooo boring. They've got even more rules than informal ones. You might need to know how to write one if you do a job application or a letter of complaint for one of your writing tasks.

Get the layout and language right

The name and address of who you're writing to goes here.

If you don't know the person's name, write here "Muy señor mío: / Muy señora mía:". Remember to follow the greeting with a colon (:) and not a comma (,). If you do know the person's name, write "Estimado señor García:" or "Estimada señora García:".

Yours faithfully

Hotel Gobi
Calle Altamirano 220
Granada
Spain

Rebecca Horwich
16 Peel Street
Guildford
Reino Unido
3 de agosto de 2009

Muy señor mío:

Pasé diez días en su hotel en junio, y le escribo para informarle de unos problemas que tuve. El aire acondicionado en mi habitación no funcionaba, y hacía mucho calor. El cuarto de baño estaba sucio. Además, la recepcionista era muy antipática. Quisiera un reembolso porque estoy muy decepcionada.

Le saluda atentamente

R Horwich

Rebecca Horwich

Put your name and address up here.

Put the date over here.

This lot means: I spent ten days in your hotel in June, and I'm writing to tell you about some problems that I had. The air conditioning in my room wasn't working, and it was very hot. The bathroom was dirty. Also, the receptionist was very unfriendly. I would like a refund because I'm very disappointed.

Use lots of fancy phrases in formal letters

Use these phrases to turn your formal letters from drab to fab.

No dude en contactarme si necesita más información. = Don't hesitate to contact me if you need any more information.

Dándole las gracias por anticipado. = Thank you in advance.

If you have to write apologising for something, use 'disculparse'.

Quisiera disculparme por no haberle respondido antes. = I would like to apologise for not having replied to you sooner.

the mistake: el error
the problem: el problema

How to end a formal letter — just stop writing...

Practice, practice, practice — that's what GCSE Spanish is all about. You'll pick up lots of marks if you can write in a formal style without sounding like you've just learnt a few stock phrases. So get going now — the more letters you write, the more natural the phrases are going to sound.

Revision Summary

This section is all the absolute basics. You need to know all this backwards by the time you get into the exams. All the bits on your opinions, and on times (including today, tomorrow, every week, on Mondays etc.) can make a huge difference to your marks. The best way to check you know it all is to do all these questions — if you get stuck or get it wrong, go back over the section and have another try at the questions until you get them right every time.

1) Count out loud from 1 to 20 in Spanish.

2) How do you say these numbers in Spanish? a) 22 b) 35 c) 58 d) 71 e) 112 f) 2101

3) What are these in Spanish? a) 1st b) 2nd c) 5th d) 10th e) 25th

4) What do these words mean? a) cada b) unos

5) Ask 'What time is it?' in Spanish.
Look at your watch, and say what time it is, out loud and in Spanish.

6) How would you say these times in Spanish? a) 5.00 b) 10.30 c) 13.22 d) 16.45

7) Say all the days of the week in Spanish, from Monday to Sunday.

8) How do you say these in Spanish? a) yesterday b) today c) tomorrow

9) Say all of the months of the year, from January to December in Spanish.

10) How do you say the date of your birthday in Spanish?

11) '¿Qué haces esta noche?' means 'What are you doing tonight?'
How would say 'What are you doing a) this morning?' b) this afternoon?' c) next week?'

12) 'Practico pocas veces el deporte' means 'I seldom do sport.'
How would you say: a) 'I do sport every day.' b) 'I often do sport.'
c) 'I sometimes do sport.'

13) 'Cantas' means 'You sing' or 'You are singing'. What do these questions mean?
a) ¿Por qué cantas? b) ¿Dónde cantas? c) ¿Qué cantas?
d) ¿Cantas bien? e) ¿Cuándo cantas? f) ¿Cantas?

14) How do you say these in Spanish? a) Please b) Thank you c) How are you?

15) How would you ask someone what they think of Elvis Presley? (In Spanish.)
Give as many ways of asking it as you can.

16) How would you say these things in Spanish? Give at least one way to say each of them.
a) I like this film. b) I don't like this newspaper. c) I find this novel interesting.
d) I love this magazine. e) I find this music awful. f) I think that this team is fantastic.

17) To win this week's star prize, complete the following sentence in 10 words or less (in Spanish): 'I like Big Brother because...'

18) To win last week's rotten eggs, complete the following sentence in 10 words or less (in Spanish): 'I don't like Big Brother because...'

19) a) How would you start a letter to your friend Elena?
b) How would you end it? Give two options.

20) How would you start a letter to your bank manager, Mr Ordóñez?

Food

This page is guaranteed to get your tummy rumbling. Any of this stuff could come up in your GCSE.

La carnicería, la tienda de comestibles — Butcher's, grocer's

Meats:	la carne
beef:	la carne de vaca
pork:	la carne de cerdo
chicken:	el pollo
lamb:	el cordero
sausage:	la salchicha
ham:	el jamón
steak:	el filete
burger:	la hamburguesa
fish:	el pescado
seafood:	los mariscos
squid:	los calamares

Vegetables:	las legumbres
potato:	la patata
carrot:	la zanahoria
tomato:	el tomate
cucumber:	el pepino
onion:	la cebolla
cauliflower:	la coliflor
bean:	la judía
mushroom:	el champiñón
cabbage:	la col
lettuce:	la lechuga
pea:	el guisante

Fruits:	la fruta
apple:	la manzana
banana:	el plátano
strawberry:	la fresa
lemon:	el limón
orange:	la naranja
raspberry:	la frambuesa
peach:	el melocotón
pineapple:	la piña
pear:	la pera

Las bebidas y los postres — Drinks and desserts

Mmm, my favourite vocab — this is more like it...

Drinks:	las bebidas
beer:	la cerveza
tea:	el té
coffee:	el café
white coffee:	el café con leche
wine:	el vino
red/white wine:	el vino tinto / blanco
orange juice:	el zumo / jugo de naranja
mineral water:	el agua mineral

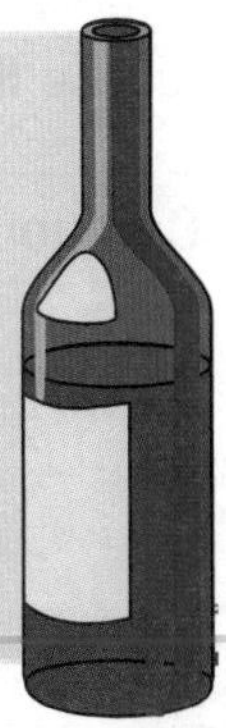

Desserts:	los postres
cake:	la tarta / el pastel
biscuit:	la galleta
ice cream:	el helado
chocolate:	el chocolate
sugar:	el azúcar
cream:	la nata
pancake:	el crep
yogurt:	el yogur
honey:	la miel
jam:	la mermelada

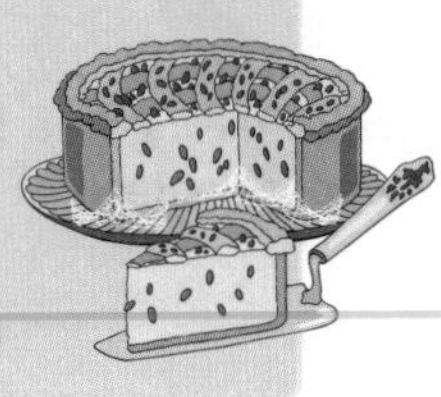

Otros alimentos — Other foods

Some absolute basics here — and some Spanish specialities that could just pop up.

bread:	el pan
milk:	la leche
egg:	el huevo
butter:	la mantequilla
cheese:	el queso
bread roll:	el panecillo
sandwich:	el bocadillo
breakfast cereals:	los cereales
chips:	las patatas fritas
crisps:	las patatas
salt:	la sal
pepper:	la pimienta
rice:	el arroz
pasta:	la pasta
soup:	la sopa

Spanish specialities:	las especialidades españolas
olives:	las aceitunas
cold tomato soup:	el gazpacho
snacks eaten in cafés and bars:	las tapas
rice dish with chicken, seafood and vegetables:	la paella
Spanish potato omelette:	tortilla española
spicy sausage:	el chorizo, el salchichón
cured ham:	el jamón serrano
thick hot chocolate with fritters:	chocolate con churros
almond nougat:	el turrón
set custard dessert:	el flan

There's some food for thought on this page...

A lot of foods are similar to the English words — like el café, el chocolate, el limón, but a lot of them aren't. You'll just have to learn them — any of them could easily come up in your reading or listening exam. Have a good look at those Spanish specialities too — they might turn up.

Food

You probably have some foods you can't stand, and others you love — well, here's how to say so.

Me gusta / Me gustan... — I like...

You can use 'me gusta' and 'no me gusta' to talk about anything you like or dislike — including food.

(No) me gusta la nata. = I (don't) like cream.

coffee: el café

(No) me gustan las manzanas. = I (don't) like apples.

bananas: los plátanos
vegetables: las verduras

No como queso. = I don't eat cheese.

never: nunca

chocolate:	chocolate
meat:	carne
squid:	calamares
nuts:	nueces

Soy vegetariano/a. = I'm a vegetarian.

vegan: vegetariano/a estricto/a

See page 13 for the names of foods.

¿Puede...? — Can you...?

Here's a dead nifty phrase to learn. Use it properly and you'll be the essence of politeness.

¿Puede pasarme la sal, por favor? = Can you pass me the salt, please?

If you're talking to a friend, use 'puedes' instead of 'puede'.

a napkin:	una servilleta
the sugar:	el azúcar
the cream:	la nata
the milk:	la leche
the pepper:	la pimienta

¿Tienes hambre o sed? — Are you hungry or thirsty?

Of course, it won't do you any good to be able to say what you like if you can't tell people you're hungry first...

¿Tienes hambre? = Are you hungry?

very hungry:	mucha hambre
thirsty:	sed
very thirsty:	mucha sed

Tengo hambre. = I'm hungry.

thirsty: sed

No gracias, no tengo hambre. = No thanks, I'm not hungry.

Are you hungry or thirsty? Or Bashful or Doc...

Make sure you can say what you like and don't like — it comes up in loads of different situations, so it's dead important. And if you say you're vegetarian or vegan, don't say you like sausages.

Mealtimes

A lot of this is useful in different situations — not just in conversations at the dinner table. There's a pretty good chance it'll come up in the listening exam, so it's the sort of stuff you really need to know.

¿Te gusta la cena? — Do you like the dinner?

You'll get asked for an opinion in most Spanish restaurants.

La comida estaba **buena**.

= The meal was good.

very good:	muy rico/a
bad:	malo/a
very bad:	muy malo/a

El desayuno estaba **delicioso***, gracias.*

= Breakfast was delicious, thanks.

La comida no estaba buena.

= The meal wasn't good.

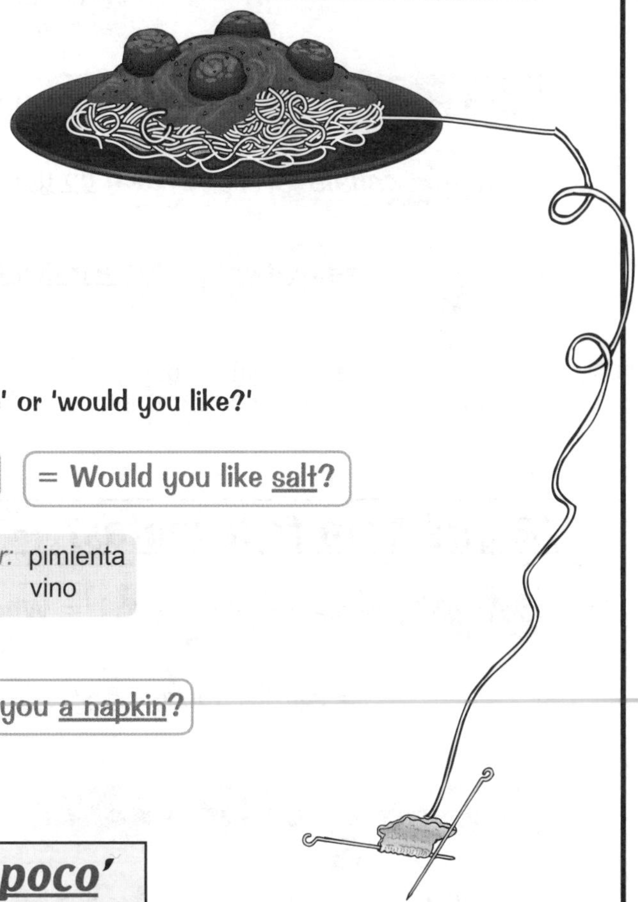

¿Quisiera...? — Would you like...?

Remember: 'Quisiera' means 'I would like' or 'you would like' or 'would you like?'

¿Quisiera tomar **sal***?*

= Would you like salt?

pepper:	pimienta
wine:	vino

the water:	el agua
the butter:	la mantequilla

¿Le puedo pasar **una servilleta***?*

= Can I pass you a napkin?

If you only want a little, ask for 'un poco'

These amount words are dead useful, and not just here...

Quisiera **mucho** *azúcar, por favor.*

= I would like lots of sugar, please.

a bit: un poco de

Quisiera **una porción grande** *de tarta.*

= I would like a big piece of cake.

He comido **bastante***, gracias.*

= I've eaten enough, thanks.

a lot: mucho

Tengo suficiente.

= I've got enough.

For more quantities info, look at page 1.

Tasty words — plenty to get your teeth into...

There's loads of really useful stuff on this page. There are zillions of situations where you'll need to say 'lots', 'not much', 'a little', etc. Scribble down those words and learn them — and don't forget the rest of the page. Spend some time practising a few sentences — it'll make all the difference.

Daily Routine

You might find it hard to imagine that anyone would ever care what time you get up, have your breakfast and have a shower. You've got to be able to talk about it though, so don't just skip it.

¿Cuándo se come...? — When do you eat...?

¿Cuándo se cena? = When do you eat dinner? *Literally: When does one eat dinner?*

What time...?: ¿A qué hora...?

eat breakfast: se desayuna / se come el desayuno
eat lunch: se almuerza / se come el almuerzo
eat dinner: se cena / se come la cena

¿Cuándo cenas? = When do you eat dinner? *(Informal, singular)*

¿Cuándo cenáis? = When do you eat dinner? *(Informal, plural)*

See page 2 for more times.

Cenamos a las siete. = We eat dinner at seven o' clock.

We eat breakfast: Desayunamos
We eat lunch: Almorzamos, Comemos

Almuerzo a la una. = I eat lunch at one.

I eat breakfast: Desayuno
I eat dinner: Ceno

¿A qué hora te levantas? — What time do you get up?

¿A qué hora te despiertas? = What time do you wake up?

get up: te levantas *go to bed:* te acuestas

Me despierto a las siete y media. = I wake up at half past seven.

I get up: Me levanto
I have a shower: Me ducho
I get dressed: Me visto
I go to bed: Me acuesto
He / She wakes up: Se despierta
They wake up: Se despiertan

See p. 104 for more on how to use these verbs.

¿Ayudas en casa? — Do you help at home?

Lavo los platos en casa. = I wash up at home.

I tidy my room: Arreglo mi cuarto
I vacuum: Paso la aspiradora

Tengo que lavar/fregar los platos. = I have to wash up.

iron: planchar
lay the table: poner la mesa

I get up at 8am. And I wake up at about 11...

There's lots to learn on this page, but it's all really useful if you need to talk about your daily routine. These phrases are great if you do a "day in the life" task for your writing assessment too.

About Yourself

Talking about yourself — well, it's my favourite subject. There are all sorts of things they could ask about — it's a good idea to have a think about how to answer some of these questions now.

Háblame de tí — Tell me about yourself

¿Cómo te llamas? = What are you called?

Me llamo Angela. = I'm called Angela.

¿Cuántos años tienes? = How old are you?

Tengo quince años. = I'm 15 years old.

¿Cuándo es tu cumpleaños? = When is your birthday?

Mi cumpleaños es el doce de diciembre. = My birthday is on the 12th December.

¿Dónde vives? = Where do you live?

Vivo en Lancaster. = I live in Lancaster.

¿Qué te gusta? = What do you like?

Me gusta el fútbol. = I like football.

¿Cómo eres? — What are you like?

Soy alto/a. = I am tall.

small: pequeño/a
slim: delgado/a
fat: gordo/a
thin: flaco/a
short (in height): bajo/a
medium height: de talla mediana

Tengo los ojos azules. = I have blue eyes

brown: marrones
green: verdes

Tengo el pelo largo. = I have long hair

short: corto
shoulder-length: a media melena
quite long: bastante largo
dark: moreno
black: negro
light brown: castaño
blonde/fair: rubio
straight: liso
curly: rizado

I'm red-haired: soy pelirrojo/a

For more colours see page 35.

¿Cómo se escribe? — How do you spell that?

Here's how to pronounce the letters of the Spanish alphabet. Practise going through it out loud — yes, you'll sound daft, but you'd sound dafter getting it wrong.

A — a (like 'cat')	H — **ach**ay ('ch' like child)	Ñ — **en**yay	U — ooh
B — bay	I — ee (like 'me')	O — o (like 'pot')	V — **ooh**bay
C — thay* (like 'think')	J — **ho**ta ('h' like 'loch')	P — pay	W— **ooh**bay **do**blay
D — day	K — ka (like 'cat')	Q — koo	X — **e**kis
E — ay (like 'day')	L — **e**lay	R — **e**ray	Y — ee gree-**ay**ga
F — **e**fay	M — **e**may	S — **es**say	Z — **thay**ta*
G — hay ('h' like 'loch')	N — **e**nay	T — tay	

*In southern Spain and Latin America, they say these as C — say and Z — sayta.

Enough about me, let's talk about... me again...

Talking about yourself isn't a chore — it's just practice. The alphabet's a bit of a pain though.

Family, Friends and Pets

Zzzzz... Families and pets... How boring... Still — there are marks to be won I suppose.

Tengo una hermana — I have one sister

This is pretty easy — just learn the words for different family members and then slot in their names.

Mi madre se llama Sue. = My mother is called Sue.

The average family

My father:	Mi padre
My brother:	Mi hermano
My sister:	Mi hermana
My aunt:	Mi tía
My uncle:	Mi tío
My cousin:	Mi primo/a
My grandmother:	Mi abuela
My grandfather:	Mi abuelo
My friend:	Mi amigo/a
My boy/girlfriend:	Mi novio/a
My stepfather:	Mi padrastro
My stepmother:	Mi madrastra
My stepbrother:	Mi hermanastro
My stepsister:	Mi hermanastra

Tengo dos hermanas. = I have two sisters.

Mis hermanas se llaman Louise y Laura. = My sisters are called Louise and Laura.

If you're talking about more than one person, use "se llaman", not "se llama".

Have a bash at describing some of your family members too:

Tiene doce años. = He/She's 12 years old.

Son bajos. = They are short.

Tiene el pelo liso. = He/She has straight hair.

Tiene los ojos azules. = He/She has blue eyes.

¿Tienes animales? — Do you have any pets?

Even if you don't have any pets, you still need to learn this stuff.
Otherwise you'll kick yourself if you get a question on it in your listening or reading exam.

Tengo un perro. = I have a dog.

a cat:	un gato
a bird:	un pájaro
a rabbit:	un conejo
a mouse:	un ratón
a horse:	un caballo
a guinea pig:	una cobaya

Es amarillo. = He is yellow.

Practise using different descriptive words.

Mi perro se llama Enrique. = My dog is called Enrique.

See page 35 for colours and page 17 for things like fat and thin.

My dog's called Rocky — he's a Boxer...

Questions about family can get you some easy marks — if you know your stuff. Learning this stuff will give you a big head start — practising it will make your chances of doing well even better.

Personality

The more description you can give about people's personality in Spanish, the better.
Just writing "My mum is nice. My dad is nice. My friend is nice..." is too boring for words.

¿Cómo es ...? — What's ... like?

Mi mejor amiga **es** *inteligente*. = My best friend (female) is intelligent.

My best friend (male):	Mi mejor amigo
My mum:	Mi mamá
My dad:	Mi papá
My Spanish teacher:	Mi profesor(a) de español

very intelligent:	muy inteligente
creative:	creativo/a
outgoing:	extrovertido/a
funny:	gracioso/a

Mis padres **son** *responsables*. = My parents are responsible.

My brothers and sisters:	Mis hermanos
My aunt and uncle:	Mis tíos
My grandparents:	Mis abuelos
My friends (male and female):	Mis amigos
My friends (female only):	Mis amigas

strict:	estrictos/as
friendly:	amables

La personalidad — Personality

GOOD QUALITIES: LAS CUALIDADES

friendly:	amable, amistoso/a	*confident:*	seguro/a de sí mismo/a	*daring:*	atrevido/a
nice:	simpático/a	*optimistic:*	optimista	*ambitious:*	ambicioso/a
cheerful:	alegre, feliz	*honest:*	sincero/a, honesto/a	*strong:*	fuerte
funny:	cómico/a, gracioso/a	*honourable:*	honrado/a	*sporty:*	deportivo
generous:	generoso/a	*patient:*	paciente	*active:*	activo/a
polite:	formal, bien educado/a, cortés	*affectionate:*	cariñoso/a	*independent:*	independiente
good-looking:	guapo/a	*talkative:*	hablador(a)	*intelligent:*	inteligente
understanding:	comprensivo/a	*tolerant:*	tolerante	*creative:*	creativo/a
sensitive:	sensible	*responsible:*	responsable	*outgoing:*	extrovertido/a
		sensible:	prudente	*introverted:*	introvertido/a
		serious:	serio/a	*quiet:*	callado/a
		brave:	valiente	*reserved:*	reservado/a
				shy:	tímido/a

BAD QUALITIES: LOS DEFECTOS

aggressive:	agresivo/a	*selfish:*	egoísta	*cowardly:*	cobarde
impatient:	impaciente	*mean/stingy:*	avaro/a	*jealous:*	celoso/a
unfriendly:	antipático/a	*pessimist:*	pesimista	*weak:*	débil
lazy:	perezoso/a, vago/a	*clumsy:*	torpe	*highly strung:*	nervioso/a
		greedy:	glotón	*arrogant:*	orgulloso/a

I've got a great personality — and 4 horrid ones...

You don't need to be able to say all these words in Spanish — just the ones that fit in with your writing and speaking tasks. Make sure you can recognise and understand everything though.

Relationships and Future Plans

Here's your chance to talk about who you get on with and who you could happily throw down a well.

Me llevo bien con ... — I get on well with ...

"(No) me llevo bien con..." is a really handy phrase if you're asked to talk about relationships with your family and friends. For extra marks, say why you do or don't get on with them.

Me llevo bien con mi madre porque es muy simpática. = I get on well with my mother because she's very nice.

very well:	muy bien
brilliantly:	estupendamente
badly:	mal
dreadfully:	fatal

You can use any of the personality words from p. 19.

No me llevo bien con mi padre porque es estricto. = I don't get on well with my father because he's strict.

my stepfather:	mi padrastro
my grandfather:	mi abuelo
my brother:	mi hermano

Me llevo bien con mis hermanos, pero a veces nos peleamos. = I get on well with my brothers and sisters, but we sometimes argue.

friends: amigos

Planes para el futuro — Plans for the future

Use 'me gustaría' to say what you'd like to do in the future.

Dentro de diez años me gustaría casarme. = In ten years I'd like to get married.

In fifteen years:	Dentro de quince años
In the future:	En el futuro
One day:	Algún día

have a child:	tener un hijo
buy a house:	comprarme una casa

Cuando tenga treinta años me gustaría tener un hijo. = When I'm thirty I'd like to have a child.

This is the subjunctive. See p. 106 for more on how to use it.

twenty-one:	veintiún
twenty-six:	veintiséis
thirty-five:	treinta y cinco
forty:	cuarenta

No quiero casarme nunca. = I never want to get married.

I don't like relationships — I get sea sick...

Saying who you don't get on with and why is pretty satisfying. The stuff about future plans is tricky, but you'll look clever if you use the future correctly in the speaking or writing tasks.

Social Issues and Equality

Talking about this kind of thing can seem daunting enough in English, let alone in Spanish.
They love social issues though, so learning all this stuff could earn you a whole heap of marks.

El paro / el desempleo — Unemployment

Unemployment is rubbish, but you might have to talk about it or at least understand it. Here goes...

Hay mucha gente en paro en la ciudad. = There are lots of unemployed people in the town.

not many: poca gente
the area: la región *the village:* el pueblo

El desempleo en Gran Bretaña es un gran problema hoy en día. = Unemployment in Britain is a big problem nowadays.

Nadie tiene problemas en encontrar trabajo. = Nobody has a problem finding work.

La igualdad de derechos — Equal Rights

This is your chance for a good rant, in Spanish of course.

Creo que la igualdad de derechos es muy importante. = I think equal rights are very important.

are unimportant: no es muy importante

A veces hay discriminación contra los extranjeros. = There's sometimes discrimination against foreign people.

women: las mujeres
immigrants: los inmigrantes

sexist: sexista
unfair: injusto

Me parece racista. = It seems racist to me.

Eso me molesta. = That annoys me.

La presión del grupo — Peer Pressure

Peer pressure now — the fun never ends on this page, does it?

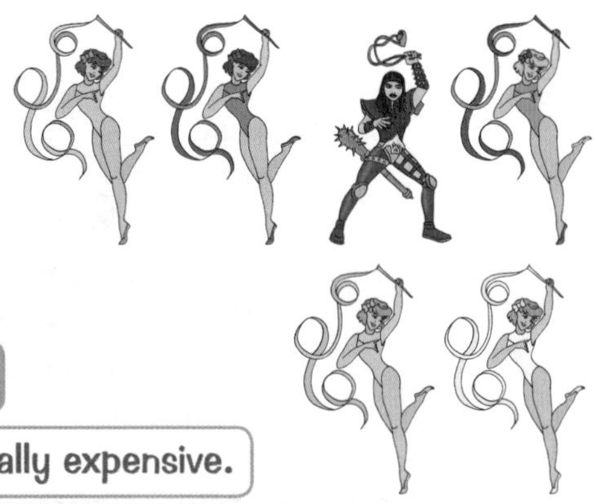

Me parece difícil conservar la individualidad. = I think it's difficult to stay a true individual.

Uno siempre tiene que llevar ropa de moda y es muy cara. = You always have to wear fashionable clothing and it's really expensive.

If you want to avoid peer pressure, stop peering...

Maybe you'll be lucky and you won't actually need any of this stuff for any of your exams. There's a good chance you'll be unlucky though, so you'd better learn it to be on the safe side. Sorry.

Feeling Unwell

If your speaking or writing task's about being ill on holiday, then this is the page for you. Even if you're not doing it for a speaking or writing task, this stuff is still useful for reading and listening.

¿Está bien? — Are you OK?

If you're feeling ill (or pretending to for one of your speaking tasks) you need to be able to say so.

Estoy enfermo/a. = I am ill.

Me siento mal. = I feel ill.

Necesito ir al médico. = I need to go to the doctor's.

to the hospital: al hospital
to the chemist's: a la farmacia

¿Qué le duele? — What hurts?

Use 'me duele...' or 'tengo dolor de...' to say which bit hurts. You need to use 'el' or 'la' before the body part when you use 'me duele...' — with 'tengo dolor de...' you don't.

Me duele el dedo. = My finger hurts.

hurt (plural): duelen

my head: la cabeza
my ears: los oídos

Remember to use 'el' or 'la' with body parts in Spanish — not 'mi' or 'mis'.

Estoy resfriado/a. = I have a cold.

Tengo dolor de estómago. = I have stomach ache.

a headache: dolor de cabeza
a sore throat: dolor de garganta
sunstroke: una insolación
a temperature: fiebre *(fem)*
flu: gripe *(fem)*

You can use 'tengo dolor de' with any part of your body that's hurting.

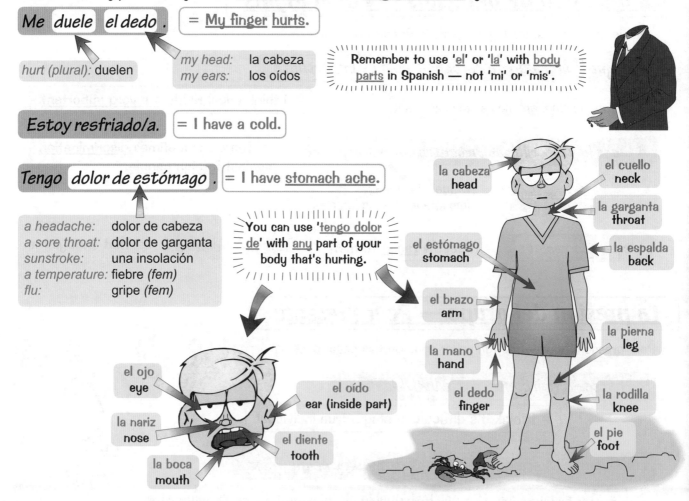

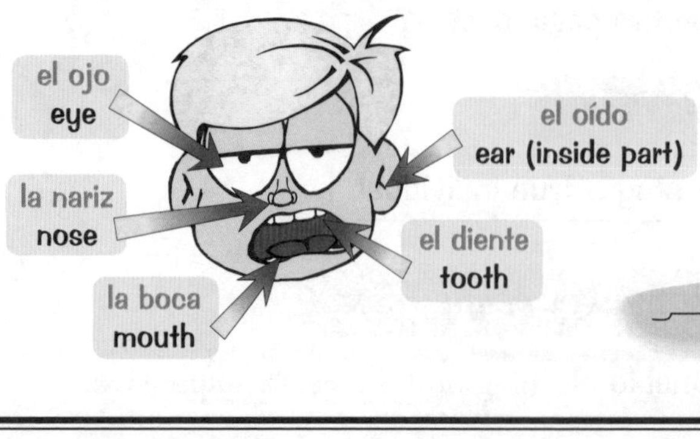

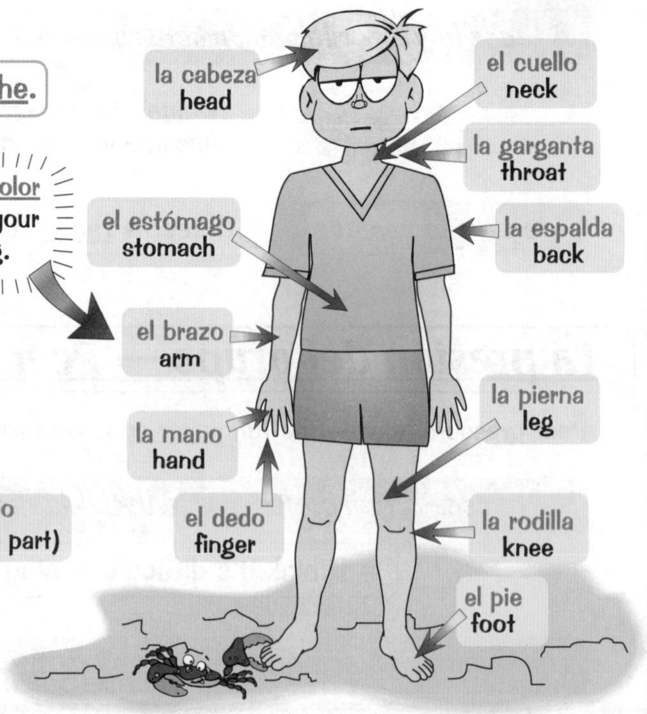

Going to the doctor's — it's a pain in the neck...

You know the score — practise using these phrases as much as you can. If you know 'em well, you won't get 'em wrong. This stuff's all really useful for if you ever actually feel ill on holiday — unless of course you're in Germany or France or somewhere, in which case it'll be no use at all.

Health and Health Issues

¡Qué bueno! — PSHE in Spanish, you lucky, lucky thing.

La dieta — Diet

No, I'm not talking about any ridiculous lettuce-only, weight loss diet.
This is about your normal everyday diet and how healthy it is, or isn't.

¿Comes bien? = Do you eat well?

Sí, como mucha fruta. = Yes, I eat lots of fruit.

No, como patatas fritas casi todos los días. = No, I eat chips almost every day.

El ejercicio — Exercise

It doesn't matter if you don't do any, just be able to say so.

¿Qué haces para mantenerte en buena salud? = What do you do to stay healthy?

Juego al fútbol y al tenis regularmente. = I regularly play football and tennis.

No hago nada. Nunca hago ejercicio. = I don't do anything. I never exercise.

¿Qué piensas del fumar? — What do you think of smoking?

Creo que el fumar es un hábito horrible. = I think smoking is a horrible habit.

Sé que no es muy sano, pero me parece muy elegante fumar. = I know it's unhealthy, but I think it's very stylish to smoke.

Nunca fumaría porque no quiero llegar a ser adicto/a. = I would never smoke because I don't want to become addicted.

(I would) drink alcohol: bebería alcohol
(I would) take drugs: tomaría drogas
(I would) inject drugs: me inyectaría drogas

an alcoholic: alcohólico/a
a drug addict: drogadicto/a
HIV positive: seropositivo/a
ill: enfermo/a

Problemas de salud — Health problems

El alcohol puede dañar el hígado. = Alcohol can damage your liver.

(passive) smoking: El fumar (pasivo)
drugs: Las drogas (pueden)
junk food: La comida basura

your heart: el corazón
your lungs: los pulmones
your brain: el cerebro

El fumar puede provocar un ataque cardíaco. = Smoking can cause a heart attack.

breathing problems: problemas respiratorios

But can Spanish revision cause a brain attack...

There is loads you might want to say about these exciting things, but learning the stuff on this page is a good start. Think about what else you might want to say, write it down, and practise it.

Revision Summary

Phew, there's a lot to learn in this section. All the vocab lists might seem daunting, but vocab's the most straightforward thing to learn — just keep testing yourself until you're sure of everything. Boring but effective. Once you think you've got everything, have a go at these delightful questions — that's sure to cheer you up.

1) How do you say these foods in Spanish? Don't forget 'el' or 'la'.
   a) potato b) ham c) orange d) wine e) ice cream f) egg g) rice
2) Name four typical Spanish foods.
3) How would you ask your Spanish friend Miguel if he likes carrots? (Miguel doesn't speak English).
4) Miguel offers you a burger. How would you say:
   a) Thank you, I like burgers.
   b) I'm a vegetarian.
   c) No thanks, I'm not hungry.
5) How would you tell Miguel that you would like:
   a) lots of milk in your coffee.
   b) a big portion of Spanish omelette.
6) ¿A qué hora cenas?
7) Describe your daily routine in Spanish. Mention at least three things that you do and say when you do them.
8) ¿Cómo te llamas?
9) ¿Cuántos años tienes?
10) You get a letter from your Mexican pen pal Susana. She includes this description of herself:
    Soy baja y bastante delgada. Tengo el pelo largo y negro. Tengo los ojos marrones.
    Write out the description of Susana in English.
11) Describe yourself in Spanish.
12) Say (out loud) how to spell your name in Spanish.
13) What do these Spanish words mean? a) el hermano b) la abuela c) el padrastro
14) Make a list of ten good qualities in Spanish, and five bad qualities.
15) How do you say 'I get on well with my sister' in Spanish?
16) What does 'Cuando tenga veintiocho años me gustaría casarme' mean?
17) Write a sentence about unemployment in Spanish. Any sentence you like.
18) What are the two ways of saying you're not very well in Spanish?
19) Write out the following body parts in Spanish: a) head b) stomach c) nose.
20) What do the following words mean? a) el brazo b) la boca c) la garganta
21) ¿Qué haces para mantenerte en buena salud?
22) How do you say 'passive smoking can cause breathing problems' in Spanish?

Sports and Hobbies

I was never much cop at sport — I could never remember the vocab. OK, maybe you don't need to know it perfectly, but you've got to be able to recognise these words if they turn up.

¿Practicas algún deporte? — Do you play any sports?

NAMES OF SPORTS

football:	el fútbol
basketball:	el baloncesto
swimming:	la natación
tennis:	el tenis
table tennis:	el tenis de mesa, el ping pong
squash:	el squash
hockey:	el hockey
athletics:	el atletismo
boxing:	el boxeo
skating:	el patinaje
skateboarding:	el monopatinaje

VERBS FOR SPORTS

to run:	correr	*to walk, hike:*	hacer senderismo
to cycle:	hacer ciclismo	*to go climbing:*	hacer alpinismo
to swim:	nadar	*to do aerobics:*	hacer aerobic
to play football:	jugar al fútbol	*to go for a walk:*	dar un paseo
to play tennis:	jugar al tenis	*to go fishing:*	ir de pesca
to jog:	hacer footing	*to ski:*	esquiar, hacer esquí

PLACES YOU CAN DO SPORTS

sports centre:	el polideportivo	*gym:*	el gimnasio
leisure centre:	el centro de deportes	*park:*	el parque
swimming pool:	la piscina	*ice rink:*	la pista de hielo
sports field:	el campo de deportes		

MORE SPORTY WORDS

ball:	la pelota
match:	el partido

Mi deporte preferido es el boxeo. = My favourite sport is boxing.

Me gusta hacer alpinismo. = I like going climbing.

¿Tienes un pasatiempo? — Do you have a hobby?

Strewth — more flippin' lists. This time it's hobbies. Same thing applies — you won't need them all, but any one of them could turn up... But first off learn the ones that apply to hobbies you do.

GENERAL BUT VITAL

hobby:	el pasatiempo
interest:	el interés
club:	un club (de...)
member:	el/la miembro

OTHER IMPORTANT NOUNS

chess:	el ajedrez
film:	la película
performance:	la sesión
play (in a theatre):	la obra de teatro
game:	el juego

VERBS FOR OTHER ACTIVITIES

to dance:	bailar
to sing:	cantar
to collect:	coleccionar
to read:	leer
to play (an instrument):	tocar

MUSICAL INSTRUMENTS

violin:	el violín
flute:	la flauta
drum kit:	la batería
clarinet:	el clarinete
guitar:	la guitarra
trumpet:	la trompeta
piano:	el piano
cello:	el violoncelo

MUSICAL WORDS

band, group:	el grupo	*instrument:*	el instrumento
CD:	el CD, el disco compacto	*concert:*	el concierto
		stereo:	el estéreo

Toco la guitarra en un grupo. = I play the guitar in a band.

Juego al ajedrez. = I play chess.

My hobby is revising Spanish...

Sport and hobbies are common enough topics, so learn as much of this vocab as you can. Even if you hate sport, you still need to have a good idea of what things mean — you'll kick yourself if you skip it and then end up getting a question on sport in your reading or listening exam.

Sports and Hobbies

Free time activities are bound to come up one way or another at GCSE. You have to be able to say what you get up to, and give opinions on other hobbies. It's must-learn stuff.

¿Qué haces en tu tiempo libre? — What do you do in your free time?

Practise writing some of your own sentences about your free time.

Los fines de semana juego al fútbol. = I play football at weekends.

Every day:	Todos los días
Every week:	Todas las semanas
Twice a month:	Dos veces al mes

badminton:	al bádminton
tennis:	al tenis

'To play' is 'jugar a' for sports and 'tocar' for instruments.

Colecciono sellos. = I collect stamps.

dolls:	muñecas
books:	libros

Toco el piano. = I play the piano.

the guitar:	la guitarra
the trumpet:	la trompeta

Soy miembro de un club de tenis. = I'm a member of a tennis club.

chess club:	club de ajedrez
squash club:	club de squash
football team:	equipo de fútbol

'Miembro' stays the same whether you're a girl or a boy — don't change it to 'miembra'.

¿Te gusta el fútbol? — Do you like football?

Here's how to say what you think of different hobbies — good phrases to know even if you don't really care.

Creo que el fútbol es aburrido. = I think football's boring.

the cinema:	el cine
hiking:	el senderismo

exciting:	emocionante
interesting:	interesante

Sí, me encanta el fútbol. = Yes, I love football.

No me gusta correr porque es cansado. = I don't like running because it's tiring.

Does biting your nails count as a hobby...

I don't know about you, but whenever anyone asks me what my hobbies are, my mind just goes completely blank. Learn all this stuff and you won't have the same embarrassing problem.

TV and Films

Everyone likes TV, so it shouldn't be too dull to talk about it in Spanish.

Tipos de programas — Types of programmes

¿Qué tipo de películas te gusta ver? = What type of films do you like to watch?

programmes: programas

Me gusta ver películas de ciencia ficción. = I like watching science fiction films.

crime: policíacas
romantic: románticas
adventure: de aventura
action: de acción

Me gusta ver comedias. = I like watching comedies.

game shows: programas concursos
cartoons: dibujos animados
soaps: telenovelas

¿Tienes un programa preferido? — Do you have a favourite programme?

favourite film: película preferida

¿Cuál es tu programa preferido? = What's your favourite programme?

Mi programa preferido es Gran Hermano. = My favourite programme is Big Brother.

¿Te gusta Dragon's Den? = Do you like Dragon's Den?

Sí, me encanta. = Yes, I love it.

No, no me gusta nada. = No, I don't like it at all.

¿A qué hora empieza el programa? = What time does the programme start?

the film: la película

WATCH OUT — it's el programa NOT la... Don't get it wrong.

El programa empieza a las ocho y termina a las nueve y media. = The programme starts at eight and finishes at half past nine.

I like watching soaps — good clean fun...

Whether you're always glued to Home and Away, or you're more of a Newsnight fan, you need to be able to say it in Spanish. Don't forget that TV could crop up in reading and listening too.

Talking About the Plot

If you've got to talk about a film, play or book in your writing or speaking assessment, you won't have much to say if you don't learn this lovely lot.

¿Qué películas has visto últimamente? — What films have you seen recently?

Half the fun of going to the pictures is telling your mates about it:

Hace poco vi 'Volver'. = I saw 'Volver' recently.

Last week: La semana pasada
Two weeks ago: Hace dos semanas
A month ago: Hace un mes

I read: leí

the new Spielberg film: la nueva película de Spielberg
the new novel by Jodi Picoult: la nueva novela de Jodi Picoult

¿De qué se trata la película? — What's the film about?

En la película, un francés viaja a Argentina para estudiar español. = In the film, a French man travels to Argentina to study Spanish.

the novel: la novela

three friends rob a bank: tres amigos roban un banco
a waiter kills his boss: un camarero mata a su jefe

La película se trata de una fiesta de Nochevieja. = The film is about a New Year's Eve party.

a car accident: *un accidente de tráfico*
a fight between two brides: *una pelea entre dos novias*

La historia es triste. = The story is sad.

funny: graciosa
exciting: emocionante
romantic: romántica

Al final, Susana gana un millón de dólares en la lotería. = At the end, Susana wins a million dollars on the lottery.

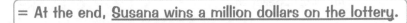

the football team loses the championship: el equipo de fútbol pierde el campeonato
the police discover the missing child: la policía descubre al niño desaparecido
the singer and the fan get married: el cantante y la aficionada se casan

I think I'm starting to lose the plot...

Talking about films in Spanish isn't quite as much fun as watching them, but at least it's not pollution or unemployment. Watching films in Spanish is great revision for the listening exam too.

Music

If you're a music fan, you've come to the right page.

¿Cómo escuchas música? — How do you listen to music?

Tengo un reproductor de mp3. = I have an mp3 player.

In Spanish, mp3 is pronounced "emay pay tres".

Escucho música en mi iPod®. = I listen to music on my iPod®.

iPod® is pronounced "ee pod".

on a stereo: en un estéreo
on the internet: por internet
on the radio: en la radio

Descargo muchos mp3. = I download lots of mp3s.

mp3 stays the same when it's plural.

Los reproductores de mp3 me parecen muy útiles porque te dejan escuchar música cuando haces footing. = I think mp3 players are really useful because they let you listen to music when you're jogging.

you're on the train: estás en el tren
you're on the bus: estás en el autobús

Gasto todo mi dinero en ir a conciertos. = I spend all my money on going to concerts.

buying CDs: comprar CDs
downloading mp3s: descargar mp3

¿Te gusta la música? — Do you like music?

Me encanta la música clásica. = I love classical music.

rock: rock
pop: pop

Three blind mice, see how they run...

Me gusta todo tipo de música. = I like all kinds of music.

jazz music: la música jazz
modern music: la música moderna
Spanish music: la música española
Coti's music: la música de Coti

rock: el rock
jazz: el jazz
rap: el rap

Mi tipo de música preferida es el flamenco. = My favourite type of music is flamenco.

No me interesa la música pop. = I'm not interested in pop music.

How do I listen to music — with my ears...

Make sure you can say what type of music you like in case you get asked. Don't forget that even though mp3 and iPod® are spelt the same in English and Spanish, they're pronounced differently.

Famous People

We're all obsessed with celebrities these days — even the exam boards, it seems.

¿Admiras a los famosos? — Do you admire celebrities?

Creo que Cheryl Cole es maravillosa. = I think Cheryl Cole is brilliant.

Es una cantante famosa del norte de Inglaterra. = She is a famous singer from the north of England.

Canta muy bien. = She sings really well.

Cheryl es muy bonita y lleva siempre ropa de moda. = Cheryl is very pretty and always wears fashionable clothes.

La vida de los famosos — Celebrity lifestyles

¿Qué hacen los famosos? = What do celebrities do?

¿Cómo es la vida de los famosos? = What are celebrities' lives like?

Ganan mucho dinero y son muy ricos. = They earn lots of money and they're very rich.

Salen en programas de televisión. = They appear on TV programmes.

Van a fiestas todas las noches. = They go to parties every night.

shopping: de compras

concerts: conciertos

Tienen que hacer entrevistas. = They have to do interviews.

La influencia de los famosos — The influence of celebrities

¿Crees que los famosos son un ejemplo positivo para los jóvenes? = Do you think celebrities are a positive example for young people?

¡Por supuesto! Tienen mucho éxito. = Of course! They're very successful.

Los admiro. = I admire them.

¡Qué va! No son normales. = No way! They're not normal.

I admire celebrities' taste in baby names...

Seriously, they come up with some of the weirdest names ever — it's almost a talent in itself. If you're doing a "day in the life of a celebrity" task, make sure you learn this page really well.

New Technology

Here's almost everything you could ever want to say about technology in Spanish, on one handy page.

¿Tienes un ordenador? — Do you have a computer?

Tengo un ordenador en casa. = I have a computer at home.

a laptop:	un ordenador portátil
broadband internet:	internet de banda ancha
satellite TV:	televisión por satélite
a mobile phone:	un (teléfono) móvil

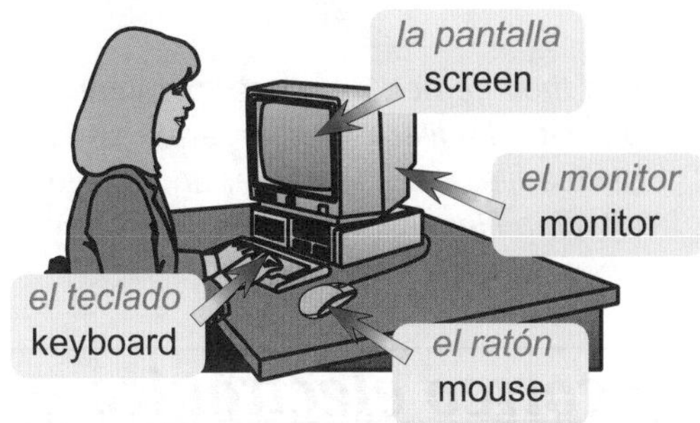

Navego por la red todos los días. = I surf the web every day.

the internet: por internet

He creado una página web sobre mi club de tenis. = I've made a web page about my tennis club.

a website:	un sitio web
a blog:	un blog

my life:	mi vida
my family:	mi familia
my favourite films:	mis películas favoritas

¿Eres aficionado/a a la nueva tecnología? — Are you a fan of new technology?

Creo que el internet es útil porque me ayuda con los deberes.

= I think the internet's useful because it helps me with my homework.

Creo que los videojuegos son una pérdida de tiempo. = I think video games are a waste of time.

the internet is: el internet es
satellite TV is: la televisión por satélite es

fun: entretenido/a/os/as

Me gusta chatear con mis amigos. = I like chatting (online) with my friends.

No me conecto a salas de chat porque la gente te puede mentir.

= I don't go on chat rooms because people can lie to you.

I can't use a computer — I'm afraid of mice...

Phew, my head's spinning after all this techno-talk. Why not take a 10-minute break from the revision and go and check your emails or update your blog or do a podcast or something.

Email and Texting

Emails and texts aren't too tricky — just learn the vocab on this page and you're away.

En el cibercafé — In the cybercafe

¿Puedo enviar un correo electrónico? = Can I send an email?

surf the internet:	navegar por internet
download a file:	descargar un archivo
save a file:	guardar un archivo
attach a file:	adjuntar un archivo

He olvidado mi contraseña. = I've forgotten my password.

Un correo electrónico — An email

Even if you don't have to write an email for a writing task, one might crop up in your reading exam.

Para: Charo <charo@correo.com> (= To)
De: Sonia <sonia@correo.com> (= From)
Asunto: Una invitación (= Subject: An invitation)

¡Hola Charo! ¿Cómo estás? Acabo de volver de un viaje a Méjico. Lo pasé muy bien. Es un país encantador. Comí muchos platos típicos de Méjico, como las fajitas y las quesadillas. ¿Te gustaría venir a mi casa para cenar este sábado? Voy a invitar a Conchi y a Marga también. Quiero contaros sobre mi viaje, y voy a preparar una cena mejicana.
Un abrazo,
Sonia

Hi Charo! How are you? I've just got back from a trip to Mexico. I had a really good time. It's a lovely country. I ate lots of typical Mexican food, like fajitas and quesadillas. Would you like to come to my house for dinner this Saturday? I'm going to invite Conchi and Marga too. I want to tell you about my trip, and I'm going to make a Mexican dinner.
Love from Sonia

If you're writing a formal email, like a job application or a letter of complaint, remember to use "usted" instead of "tú", and use the same intros and endings you'd use for a formal letter (like the one on p. 11).

Un mensaje de texto — A text message

Exam boards like to bring in new technology to show that they're "down with the kids", so don't be surprised if you have to read a text message from one of those imaginary Spanish friends in your reading exam.

17:23

Hola Bea. Voy a llegar tarde a la fiesta porque tengo que lavar los platos antes de salir. ¿Qué te vas a poner? Creo que voy a llevar mi vestido azul. Hasta pronto, Mari.

Hi Bea. I'm going to be late to the party because I have to wash the dishes before I leave. What are you going to wear? I think I'm going to wear my blue dress. See you soon, Mari.

Doesn't anybody write letters any more...

In my day, imaginary Spanish friends in exams used to write you a nice letter or card that you had to reply to. Now they just send you a rubbishy email or a text. That's progress for you.

Shopping

Whether you love it or hate it in real life, you need to know about shopping for your Spanish GCSE.

¿Dónde está...? — Where is...?

A dead handy question, this one.

¿Dónde está el supermercado, por favor? = Where is the supermarket, please?

butcher's:	la carnicería	*cake shop:*	la pastelería
baker's:	la panadería	*sweet shop:*	la confitería
grocer's:	la tienda de comestibles	*stationer:*	la papelería
chemist's:	la farmacia	*fishmonger's:*	la pescadería
newsagent:	el quiosco	*market:*	el mercado
department store:	los grandes almacenes	*delicatessen:*	la charcutería
shopping centre:	el centro comercial	*hypermarket:*	el hipermercado
book shop:	la librería	*library*	la biblioteca

The word order's the same in English and Spanish.

Remember that 'la librería' means book shop and 'la biblioteca' means library. How confusing.

Ask when shops open using '¿Cuándo...?' — 'When...?'

All very well going shopping, but let's not forget Spain is the land of siesta — opening times vary...

¿Cuándo está abierto el supermercado? = When is the supermarket open?

open (fem): abierta
shut: cerrado/a

hairdresser's: la peluquería
greengrocer's: la frutería

¿Cuándo cierra el supermercado? = When does the supermarket close?

open: abre

El supermercado cierra a las siete. = The supermarket closes at 7 pm.

¿Compras por internet? — Do you shop online?

Prefiero comprar ropa por internet porque es más cómodo. = I prefer to buy clothes on the internet because it's more convenient.

it's faster:	es más rápido
it's cheaper:	es más barato
I live far away from the shops:	vivo lejos de las tiendas

Prefiero ver las cosas antes de comprarlas. = I prefer to see things before I buy them.

Me parece inseguro comprar por internet con una tarjeta de crédito. = It seems unsafe to me to shop online with a credit card.

Shop 'til you drop...

OK, start by learning that list of lovely shops — cover 'em up, scribble 'em down and check 'em. You need to be able to recognise as many as possible — don't forget opening and closing too.

Shopping

OK, this is a page to get you started with the vocab for buying things — especially saying what you want. It's pretty darn essential, if you ask me.

La moneda española — Spanish money

Spanish money's easy. There are 100 cents in a euro, like there are 100 pence in a pound.

For numbers, see page 1.

This is what you'd see on a Spanish price tag: €5,50

This is how you say the price: *'Cinco euros, cincuenta céntimos'* = 5 euros, 50 cents

¿En qué puedo servirle? — How can I help you?

First you've got to be able to ask if the shop has what you want.

¿Tiene pan, por favor? = Excuse me, do you have any bread?

Quisiera quinientos gramos de azúcar, por favor. = I'd like 500g of sugar, please.

1kg: un kilo

¿Algo más? = Anything else?

No, gracias. = No, thank you.

Sí, por favor, también quisiera una patata. = Yes, I'd like a potato as well, please.

Tiendas de ropa — Clothes shops

Quisiera unos pantalones. = I'd like a pair of trousers.

¿Qué talla tiene usted? = What (clothes) size are you?

Mi talla es la cuarenta y dos. = I'm a size 42.

¿Qué número de zapato calza? = What shoe size are you?

Mi número de zapato es el treinta y nueve. = I'm a size 39.

CONTINENTAL SIZES

size: la talla
shoe size: el número de zapato
dress size 10 / 12 / 14 / 16...: 38 / 40 / 42 / 44...
shoe size 5 / 6 / 7 / 8 / 9 / 10...: 38 / 39 / 40 / 41 / 42 / 43...

Show me the money...

Saying what you want is an absolutely vital thing to learn. The sizes are a bit of a hassle, but they're essential if you want to buy clothes in Spain, and they might come up in your GCSE too.

Shopping

Ah the roar of the crowds, the push of the queues — we all have to shop sometime... often in the exams.

¿De qué color? — What colour?

Colours go after the noun, and agree with it (most end in 'a' if the noun's feminine and 's' or 'es' if it's plural).

COLOURS — LOS COLORES

black:	negro/a	*brown:*	marrón	*light blue:*	azul claro
white:	blanco/a	*grey:*	gris	*dark blue:*	azul oscuro
red:	rojo/a	*orange:*	naranja	*pale blue:*	azul pálido
yellow:	amarillo/a	*pink:*	rosa	*bright blue:*	azul vivo
green:	verde	*purple:*	morado/a		
blue:	azul	*violet:*	violeta		

Quisiera una falda roja. = I'd like a red skirt.

some blue trousers: unos pantalones azules
a yellow jacket: una chaqueta amarilla

Watch out — if you use colours like 'light blue' or 'bright pink', they always stay in the masculine singular.

Estoy buscando unos zapatos azul claro. = I'm looking for some light blue shoes.

a bright purple skirt: una falda morado vivo
a pale yellow dress: un vestido amarillo pálido
some dark brown trousers: unos pantalones marrón oscuro

¿Lo quiere? — Do you want it?

To buy or not to buy — that is the question... and here are the answers...

Lo quiero. = I'll take it.
It (feminine): La

Me lo quedo. = I'll take it.
it (feminine): la

No lo quiero. No me gusta el color. = I don't want it. I don't like the colour.

It's too small for me: Me queda pequeño/a.
It's too long for me: Me queda largo/a.
It's too expensive: Es demasiado caro/a.

Me queda bien. = It fits me.

Me encanta. = I love it.

Quiero devolver esta falda — I want to return this skirt

Know your rights — here's how to return faulty items.

La falda está rasgada. = The skirt is ripped.
has a hole in it: tiene un agujero

Falta un botón en la camisa. = There's a button missing on the shirt.

an exchange: un cambio

Quisiera un reembolso. = I'd like a refund.

¿Tiene el recibo? = Do you have the receipt?

This doughnut has a hole in it — I want a refund...

The trick with shopping is knowing the basic vocab first — it's a nightmare trying to bluff your way through your GCSE if you don't know the words. Practise these phrases with different vocab.

Shopping

More vocab, I'm afraid — but it's all everyday stuff that turns up frequently. Apart from clothes, there's a bit of vocab for pocket money and sales... Oh the thrills...

La ropa — Clothes

Me gusta este vestido. = I like this dress.

Los vaqueros están muy de moda. = Jeans are very fashionable.

Tracksuits:	Los chándals
Tights:	Las medias

out of fashion: pasados/as de moda

MORE CLOTHES

shirt:	la camisa	*socks:*	los calcetines	*tie:*	la corbata	*shoes:*	los zapatos
trousers:	los pantalones	*hat:*	el sombrero	*coat:*	el abrigo	*shorts:*	los pantalones cortos
dress:	el vestido	*T-shirt:*	la camiseta	*jeans:*	los vaqueros	*raincoat:*	el impermeable
skirt:	la falda	*suit:*	el traje	*tracksuit:*	el chándal	*boots:*	las botas
jumper:	el jersey, el suéter	*jacket:*	la chaqueta	*gloves:*	los guantes	*tights:*	las medias

Las rebajas — The sales

Advanced shopping vocab for advanced shoppers — and for picking up extra vocab cred.

Hay rebajas en los grandes almacenes. = There's a sale on in the department store.

Los zapatos se venden con un veinte por ciento de descuento. = There's 20% off shoes.

Compré un vestido a mitad de precio. = I bought a dress for half price.

El dinero de bolsillo — Pocket money

Recibo cinco libras de dinero de bolsillo por semana. = I get £5 pocket money a week.

£3:	tres libras
£10:	diez libras

month: mes

Gasto mi dinero de bolsillo en CDs. = I spend my pocket money on CDs.

clothing:	ropa	*computer games:*	juegos de ordenador
books:	libros	*sweets:*	caramelos

My pocket money's never in my pocket for long...

Never forget your clothes — it's common sense really. Fortunately, some of them are dead easy — el jersey, el sombrero etc. Others need a bit more effort to learn — but they'll come in handy.

Inviting People Out

A brief guide to having fun: 1) get someone to agree to do something fun, 2) decide when and where to meet. The tricky bit is you have to do it in Spanish...

¿Te apetece salir? — Do you feel like going out?

Here's one way to suggest a trip out:

Vamos **a la piscina**. = Let's go to the swimming pool.

to the theatre:	al teatro
to the park:	al parque

No, gracias. = No, thank you.

Sí, me encantaría. = Yes, I'd love to.

Good idea:	Buena idea.
Great!:	¡Estupendo!

It's always good to give a reason if you say no:

I'm sorry:	Lo siento.
I can't swim:	No sé nadar.
I don't have enough money:	No tengo bastante dinero.
I have to do my homework:	Tengo que hacer mis deberes.

You'll pick up extra marks if you use 'preferiría' to say what you'd prefer to do:

Preferiría **jugar al fútbol**. = I'd prefer to play football.

¿Dónde nos encontramos? — Where shall we meet?

You might decide to meet in front of the town hall:

Nos vemos **delante del ayuntamiento**. = Let's meet in front of the town hall.

at your house:	en tu casa
beside the church:	al lado de la iglesia

For other places, see pages 25, 33 and 38.

¿A qué hora nos encontramos? = What time shall we meet?

Nos encontramos a **las diez**. = We'll meet at 10 o'clock.

For more about times, see pages 2–3.

half past two:	las dos y media
quarter past three:	las tres y cuarto

¡Hasta **el martes**! = See you on Tuesday!

on Monday:	el lunes
on Saturday:	el sábado

¡Hasta luego! = See you later!

¡Hasta **las diez**! = See you at ten o'clock!

at one o'clock:	la una
at half past five:	las cinco y media

Where shall we meet? At the butcher's...

Arranging a meeting looks like a tricky topic. There's quite a bit of vocab to get to grips with. Then it's practising sentences, I'm afraid. Remember to give reasons and say what you'd prefer.

Going Out

Heading out? Then buying tickets, opening times and finding where things are is essential stuff.

Ask how much it costs — '¿Cuánto cuesta?'

¿Cuánto cuesta una sesión de natación? = How much does a swimming session cost?

tennis: de tenis
cycling: de ciclismo

Cuesta un euro. = It costs 1 euro.

2 euros per hour: dos euros la hora

¿Cuándo está abierta? — When does it open?

¿Cuándo está abierta la piscina? = When is the swimming pool open?

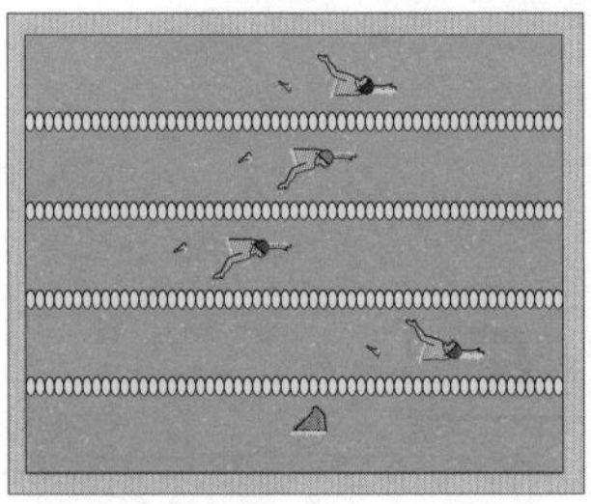

closed: cerrado/a
open: abierto/a

sports centre: el polideportivo
ice rink: la pista de hielo

Abre a las nueve y media y cierra a las cinco. = It opens at half past nine and closes at five o'clock.

Quisiera una entrada, por favor. = I'd like one ticket, please.

two tickets: dos entradas

For more times and numbers see pages 1–3.

¿Hay un cine por aquí? — Is there a cinema near here?

¿Hay un teatro por aquí? = Is there a theatre near here?

a sports field: un campo de deportes
a bowling alley: una bolera

Theatre
I wonder if there's a theatre around here.

play tennis: jugar al tenis
go for walks: pasear

¿Se puede nadar por aquí? = Can people swim near here?

Is there a Laurel and Hardy museum near here...

Nothing too problematic here — provided you learn your stuff that is... A lot of this vocab could turn up in different situations — especially in the Listening exam. It's worth learning really well.

Going Out

Blimey — lots to say here about going to the cinema or a sports match. Some of it's a bit dull, I'm afraid, but that's the price you have to pay if you want to do well. It's up to you, really.

¿Qué hiciste el fin de semana? — What did you do at the weekend?

Yep, opinions again — you've got to be able to give your thoughts.

Fui al cine y vi la nueva comedia de Jennifer Aniston. = I went to the cinema and saw Jennifer Aniston's new comedy.

a horror film: una película de miedo

¿Era buena la película? = Was the film good?

Era bastante buena. = It was quite good.

very good: muy buena
bad: mala
boring: aburrida
awful: horrible

Me encantó la película. = I loved the film.

I (really) liked: Me gustó (mucho)
I didn't like (at all): No me gustó (nada)

Un partido de fútbol — A football match

Fui al estadio para ver el partido de fútbol. = I went to the stadium to see the football match.

rugby: rugby

Vi el partido en la televisión. = I watched the match on television.

El Hull City jugó contra el Liverpool en la final de la copa. = Hull City played Liverpool in the cup final.

semi-final: la semifinal
first round: la primera vuelta

Dean Windass marcó un gol. = Dean Windass scored a goal.

two goals: dos goles

El Hull City ganó el campeonato. = Hull City won the championship.

El partido fue muy emocionante. = The match was very exciting.

boring: aburrido

My electricity goes out more than I do...

Even if you didn't do anything at the weekend apart from sit around in your pyjamas eating ice-cream, you can make something up and impress everyone with your Spanish knowledge.

Revision Summary

Now for the fun part — a chance to practise all the amazing stuff you've learnt in this section. Answer these questions without looking at the pages, then go back over the bits you're not sure of. Spanish revision's just one big party...

1) How do you say these sports in Spanish? a) football b) swimming c)tennis
2) Your Uruguayan friend Gustavo asks you, "¿Qué haces en tu tiempo libre?". What does the question mean, and how would you answer it in Spanish?
3) Your friend Nigel tells you, "En mi tiempo libre, juego al tenis, leo libros y toco la guitarra." What does this mean in English?
4) ¿Cuál es tu programa preferido? Answer in Spanish.
5) Think of a film you've seen recently and describe the plot in Spanish. (You don't need to translate the title into Spanish.)
6) How would you say in Spanish: a) I have an mp3 player b) I listen to music on the radio.
7) Write 3 sentences in Spanish about Paris Hilton and her lifestyle.
8) Carmen and Eleni are having an argument about the internet. Carmen thinks that the internet is a waste of time, but Eleni thinks that it's very useful because she can chat online with her friends in Argentina every day. Write down their conversation in Spanish.
9) In an email, what are the following in Spanish: a) To b) From c) Subject?
10) You get the following text message from your friend Paulina: "Hola. ¿Qué tal? ¿Quieres ir al parque mañana? Creo que va a hacer sol. Hasta pronto." Write out the message in English.
11) Write a reply to Paulina's text message in Spanish.
12) Ask what time the chemist's opens in Spanish.
13) Write out the following conversation in English:
    "Quisiera un vestido amarillo."
    "¿Qué talla tiene usted?"
    "Mi talla es la treinta y ocho."
14) Soledad has bought a shirt, but it's ripped and she wants to exchange it. What should she say in Spanish?
15) What are these clothes in English? a) los pantalones b) el traje c) la camiseta
16) Ana has just found out that there's 30% off clothes in the department store. How could she tell her friend Leticia about the sale in Spanish?
17) Kormi wants to see '¡Ay, Carmela!' at the cinema, but Bernard says he wants to see 'Cría cuervos'. They arrange to meet in front of the cinema at 7.30pm. Write down their conversation in Spanish.
18) Ask in Spanish what time the swimming pool closes, and say you would like two tickets.
19) Will asks Javier "¿Qué hiciste el fin de semana?" Javier says "Fui al estadio para ver un partido de rugby. Después vi una película en la televisión." Write down their conversation in English.

Holiday Destinations

First things first — if you're going to talk about holidays, you need to know the names of the countries.

Los países — Countries

Names of countries come in handy for saying where you've been on holiday, or where you'd like to go.

Learn these common countries:

Spain:	España (fem.)
England:	Inglaterra (fem.)
Scotland:	Escocia (fem.)
Wales:	País de Gales (masc.)
Ireland	Irlanda (fem.)
Northern Ireland:	Irlanda del Norte (fem.)
Great Britain:	Gran Bretaña (fem.)
United Kingdom:	Reino Unido (masc.)
France:	Francia (fem.)
Germany:	Alemania (fem.)
Italy:	Italia (fem.)
Austria:	Austria (fem.)
Holland:	Holanda (fem.)
USA:	los Estados Unidos (masc.)
Belgium:	Bélgica (fem.)
Denmark:	Dinamarca (fem.)
Norway:	Noruega (fem.)
Switzerland:	Suiza (fem.)
Sweden:	Suecia (fem.)
Russia:	Rusia (fem.)
Greece:	Grecia (fem.)
Mexico:	México / Méjico (masc.)
Peru:	Perú
Chile:	Chile
Colombia:	Colombia
Argentina:	Argentina
Cuba:	Cuba

Don't forget the continents:

Europe:	Europa (fem.)
Africa:	África (fem.)
North America:	América del Norte (fem.)
South America:	América del Sur (fem.)
Australia:	Australia (fem.)
Asia:	Asia (fem.)

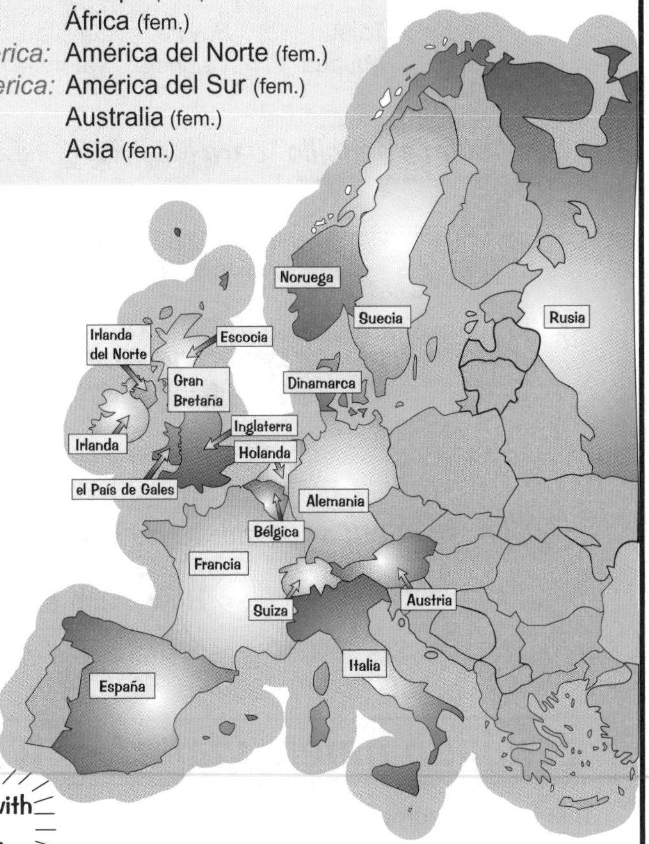

For the nationalities that go with these countries, see p. 58.

Las regiones de España — Regions of Spain

If you want to be really fancy, you can say which region of Spain you've visited.

Andalusia:	Andalucía
Aragon:	Aragón
Castile:	Castilla
Catalonia:	Cataluña
Galicia:	Galicia
Basque Country:	el País Vasco
Rioja:	La Rioja
Canary Islands:	las Islas Canarias

Andalucía está en el sur de España. = Andalusia is in the south of Spain.

north:	norte
east:	este
west:	oeste

País de Gales — no wonder it's so windy...

Knowing countries in Spanish is a good idea even if you're rubbish at geography. Look at an atlas and see how many of the countries you know in Spanish. With the ones where the Spanish word is a bit like the English, like Holland and Holanda, check you've got the spelling right too.

Catching the Train

Trains, planes and automobiles... Well, just trains for now. Learn how to talk about trains — not like a parrot, but so you can actually use the vocab.

Quisiera tomar el tren — I'd like to take the train

¿Hay un tren para Madrid? = Is there a train to Madrid?

Toledo: Toledo *Seville:* Sevilla
Malaga: Málaga *Valencia:* Valencia

Un billete sencillo para Madrid, por favor. = One single to Madrid, please.

Two: Dos
Three: Tres

single(s): billete(s) sencillo(s) / billete(s) de ida
return(s): billete(s) de ida y vuelta

Quisiera un billete de primera clase. = I'd like a first class ticket.

second class: de segunda clase

¿Cuánto cuesta un billete de ida y vuelta de segunda clase?

= How much does a second class return ticket cost?

¿Cuándo quiere viajar? — When do you want to travel?

This is more complicated, but important. You won't get far (in Spain or your exams) without it.

Quisiera ir a Santander el sábado. = I would like to go to Santander on Saturday.

today: hoy *next Monday:* el lunes que viene *on the tenth of June:* el diez de junio

¿Cuándo sale el tren para Santander? = When does the train leave for Santander?

¿Cuándo llega el tren a Santander? = When does the train arrive in Santander?

¿De qué andén sale el tren? = Which platform does the train leave from?

¿Dónde está el andén cuatro? = Where is platform four?

When does the midnight train to Georgia leave...

Learning about how to buy train tickets isn't just useful if you're on holiday in Spain or Mexico or Argentina or somewhere — it could come up in your reading and listening exams. So make sure you learn this stuff and you'll be able to handle anything they throw at you in your exam.

Catching the Train

Taking the train's one thing, but catching the metro's a whole different kettle of fish...

En la estación de metro — At the metro station

¿Qué línea necesito tomar para ir al Museo del Prado?

= What line do I need to take to go to the Prado Museum?

to the Royal Palace:	al Palacio Real
to the Plaza Mayor (main square):	a la Plaza Mayor
to the airport:	al aeropuerto

Necesita tomar la línea dos. Baje en la estación de metro 'Banco de España'.

5:	cinco
7:	siete

= You need to take line 2. Get off at 'Banco de España' station.

¿Te gusta viajar en tren? — Do you like travelling by train?

Not a great chat-up line, I admit. Here's how to give your opinion on train travel.

Vivo en Sevilla, pero tengo que viajar a menudo a Madrid. Me gusta ir en tren porque el AVE es muy rápido.

= I live in Seville, but I often have to go to Madrid. I like to go by train because the AVE* is very fast.

*El AVE and el TALGO are Spanish high-speed train services.

No me importa viajar en tren, pero prefiero viajar en avión porque es más cómodo.

= I don't mind travelling by train, but I prefer to travel by plane because it's more comfortable.

Learn this train vocab

More vocab I'm afraid... Yes, it's dull, but it's also vital to know as much as you can.

to depart:	salir	*to arrive:*	llegar	*to change (trains):*	hacer transbordo / cambiar
departure:	la salida	*arrival:*	la llegada		
the waiting room:	la sala de espera	*ticket:*	el billete	*platform:*	el andén / la vía
timetable:	el horario	*to get on:*	subir a	*ticket office:*	la taquilla
Spanish rail network:	la RENFE	*to get off:*	bajar de	*left luggage:*	la consigna
the railway:	el ferrocarril	*delay:*	el retraso		

Trains are OK, but I prefer to travel by private jet...

In real life, discussing whether or not you enjoy travelling by train is a clear sign of a very bad conversation. But Spanish GCSE isn't real life (well OK, it is, but you know what I mean) so there's nothing for it but to learn everything on this page. So what are you waiting for...

All Kinds of Transport

Here's what you need to know about other forms of transport. This is one of those topics that you'll need to know really well — and you need to know loads of vocab for it too.

¿Cómo vas? — How do you get there?

You need to say how you get about. For 'by' (e.g. by car), use 'en'. The only one that's different is 'on foot' ('a pie').

Normalmente voy **al centro** **en autobús**. = I normally go into town by bus.

to school:	al colegio
to the park:	al parque
to the swimming pool:	a la piscina

on the underground:	en el metro
by bike:	en bici (bicicleta)
by car:	en coche
by motorbike:	en moto (motocicleta)
by coach:	en autocar
by boat:	en barco
by plane:	en avión
by train:	en tren
on foot:	a pie

La salida y la llegada — Departure and arrival

Questions like this are really handy when you're travelling.

¿Hay **un autobús** *para Córdoba?* = Is there a bus to Cordoba?

a plane: un avión
a coach: un autocar

¿A qué hora sale **el próximo autobús** *para Almería?* = When does the next bus to Almería leave?

the next coach: el próximo autocar
the next boat: el próximo barco

the bus: el autobús
the coach: el autocar

¿Cuándo llega **el avión** *a Barcelona?* = When does the plane arrive in Barcelona?

¿Qué autobús...? — Which bus...?

No doubt about it — you need to be able to ask which bus or train goes where. Just learn this.

¿ **Qué autobús** *va* **al centro** *, por favor?* = Which bus goes to the town centre, please?

Which train: Qué tren
to the airport: al aeropuerto

I'm a Spanish GCSE student, get me out of here...

This stuff's pretty straightforward, really. Learn the example phrases and then you can just slot the transport vocab in to make loads of different sentences. Remember that 'on foot' is 'a pie' and all the other modes of transport are just 'en' followed by 'coche' or 'tren' or 'bicicleta' or whatever.

Planning Your Holiday

This is the kind of thing that could easily come up in your listening exam — conversations in the tourist office or the bureau de change. It could come in pretty handy if you go to Spain on holiday too.

La oficina de turismo — The tourist office

Here's how you find out what a town's got to offer.

¿Puede darme información sobre el parque zoológico, por favor?

= Can you give me information about the zoo, please?

the sights of Madrid:	los lugares de interés turístico de Madrid
the museum:	el museo
this region's typical food:	la comida típica de esta región

¿Tiene unos folletos sobre excursiones por Sevilla?

= Do you have any leaflets about excursions around Seville?

the museums in Toledo: los museos de Toledo

Quisiera visitar Aranjuez.

= I'd like to visit Aranjuez.

go to a museum:	visitar un museo
see the castle:	ver el castillo

¿Cuánto es? = How much is it?

Son treinta euros por persona. = It costs 30 euros per person.

El autocar sale del ayuntamiento a la una y media.

= The coach leaves from the town hall at half past one.

from the church:	de la iglesia
from the market:	del mercado

at 2 o'clock:	a las dos
at quarter past 3:	a las tres y cuarto

La oficina de cambio — The bureau de change

¿Puedo cambiar cien libras en euros, por favor?

= Can I change 100 pounds to euros, please?

50:	cincuenta
150:	ciento cincuenta
200:	doscientas / doscientos

dollars:	dólares
pesos:	pesos

¿Cuál es el tipo de cambio? = What's the exchange rate?

Quisiera cambiar cincuenta libras en cheques de viaje.

= I'd like to change 50 pounds to traveller's cheques.

Can I change this old tissue to euros, please...

It seems a bit mean to go on and on about holidays when you can't go on holiday because you've got your GCSEs. That's exam boards for you — mean. Well, you'll just have to grin and bear it.

Holiday Accommodation

Holidays are an exam favourite. This page has all the words you need to know about hotels, hostels, and camping. GCSEs are always full of this sort of thing, so you'd better get learning...

Las vacaciones — Holidays

Booking the right kind of room in the right kind of hotel is darned important — best learn how to do it.

General vocabulary.

holiday:	las vacaciones
abroad:	el extranjero
person:	la persona
night:	la noche

Verbs used in hotels.

to reserve:	reservar
to stay:	alojarse / quedarse
to cost:	costar
to leave:	irse

Things you might want to ask for.

room:	la habitación
double room:	la habitación doble
single room:	la habitación individual
double bed:	la cama de matrimonio
full board:	la pensión completa
half board:	la media pensión

Different kinds of accommodation.

hotel: el hotel

guest house: la pensión

campsite: el camping

historic hotel: el parador

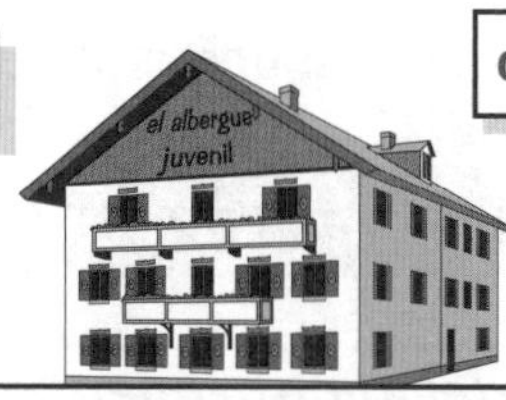

youth hostel: el albergue juvenil

More holiday vocab to learn

You may need to ask about your room, where things are in the hotel... oh, and paying the bill.

Parts of a hotel.

restaurant:	el restaurante
dining room:	el comedor
lift:	el ascensor
stairs:	la escalera
car park:	el aparcamiento
lounge:	el salón

Things about your room.

key:	la llave
balcony:	el balcón
bath:	el baño
shower:	la ducha
washbasin:	el lavabo

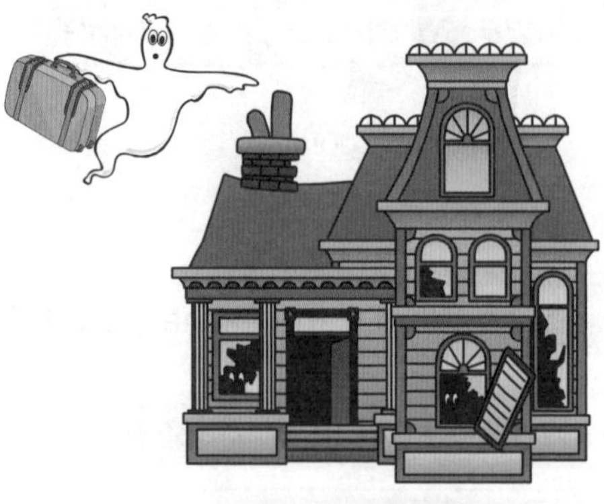

Paying for your stay.

bill:	la cuenta
price:	el precio

Extra words for camping.

tent:	la tienda
sleeping bag:	el saco de dormir
caravan:	la caravana
to camp:	acampar
pitch (noun):	la plaza
drinking water:	el agua potable

Why's it called a guest house if you have to pay...

OK, I admit this is just a load of vocabulary. If you want to really learn these words, you need to keep testing yourself until you've got it all — you need to understand this stuff if it crops up.

Booking a Room / Pitch

Learn this page if you don't want to end up sharing a room in Spain with two sweaty, cycling Swedes — or if you do. Oh and asking about rooms could come up in the exams as well.

¿Tiene una habitación libre? — Do you have a room free?

Quisiera una **habitación individual** *.* = I'd like a single room.

double room:	habitación doble
room with a bath:	habitación con baño
room with a balcony:	habitación con balcón

If you want to talk about different kinds of bookings, use the vocab you've just learned on p. 46.

Quisiera quedarme aquí **dos noches** *.* = I'd like to stay here for two nights.

one night:	una noche
one week:	una semana
a fortnight:	quince días

¿Cuánto es por noche para **una persona** *?* = How much is it per night for one person?

two people:	dos personas
four people:	cuatro personas

Vale. = OK.

Lo siento, es demasiado caro. = I'm sorry, it's too expensive.

¿Se puede acampar aquí? — Can I camp here?

Even if you're not into the outdoor life these phrases might be useful in your exams.

Quisiera una plaza para **una noche** *.* = I'd like a pitch for one night.

two nights:	dos noches
a week:	una semana
a fortnight:	quince días

a shop:	una tienda
a telephone:	un teléfono

¿Hay **agua potable** *aquí?* = Is there drinking water here?

¿Puedo hacer un fuego aquí? = Can I light a fire here?

¿Dónde está **el teléfono** *?* = Where is the telephone?

the shop:	la tienda

¿Dónde están los servicios? = Where are the toilets?

Yep, tent and shop are both 'tienda' in Spanish...

That must get confusing. I wonder if people who ask the way to the shops end up being directed to the nearest campsite. Anyway, learn everything on the page — you'll be glad you did.

Where / When is...?

Here's how to ask people where things are and how to get yourself fed. Pretty important stuff.

Ask where things are — use '¿Dónde está... ?'

Knowing how to ask where things are is very important — get these learnt.

¿Dónde está **el comedor** *, por favor?* = Where is the dining room, please?

the car park:	el aparcamiento
the games room:	la sala de juegos
the telephone:	el teléfono

See p. 46 for more things you might need to ask about.

Excuse me, where's the dining room?

Está en el **tercer piso** . = It's on the third floor.

fourth floor:	cuarto piso
second floor:	segundo piso
first floor:	primer piso
ground floor:	la planta baja

For higher floor numbers, see p. 1.

Está **al final del pasillo** . = It's at the end of the corridor.

outside:	fuera
on the left / right:	a la izquierda / derecha
straight on:	todo recto / derecho
upstairs:	arriba
downstairs:	abajo

¿Cuándo es... ? — When is... ?

Questions galore — you've met 'when' on page 4, this is just one instance where you'll need it.

¿Cuándo se sirve **el desayuno** *, por favor?* = When is breakfast served, please?

lunch:	el almuerzo / la comida
evening meal:	la cena

Se sirve a **las ocho** . = It is served at eight o'clock.

¿Hasta qué hora se sirve **la cena** ? = What time is dinner served until?

For more times, see p. 2.

Se sirve hasta las **diez y media** . = It is served until half past ten.

Actually, when is lunch? I'm starving...

The best way to check you know this stuff is to cover up the page and try to scribble the words down. After you can write the words down fine on their own, get on with writing down full sentences using them. The bits about 1st floor, 2nd floor etc. are useful for any tall buildings...

Problems with Accommodation

Holidays don't always run smoothly — even in Spanish GCSE exams.

Tengo un problema con mi habitación — I've got a problem with my room

If your luxury hotel suite turns out to be more of a flea pit, here are the phrases you need to complain.

El aire acondicionado no funciona. = The air conditioning doesn't work.

The key:	La llave
The shower:	La ducha
The telephone:	El teléfono
The television:	La televisión
The heating:	La calefacción

No hay agua caliente. = There's no hot water.

electricity:	luz
towels:	toallas

El desayuno está frío. = The breakfast is cold.

The coffee:	El café

La habitación está sucia. = The room is dirty.

smells bad:	huele mal
is too small:	es demasiado pequeña
has no window:	no tiene ventana

See p. 11 for an example of a complaint letter to a hotel.

En la comisaría — At the police station

If it's a proper holiday from hell, you might even need to go to the police station.

He perdido mi bolso. = I've lost my bag.

my passport:	mi pasaporte
my purse:	mi monedero
my money:	mi dinero
my credit card:	mi tarjeta de crédito
my keys:	mis llaves
my watch:	mi reloj
my earrings:	mis pendientes

¿Dónde perdió su bolso? = Where did you lose your bag?

Perdí mi bolso en la estación. = I lost my bag in the station.

the museum:	el museo
the cathedral:	la catedral
the shopping centre:	el centro comercial

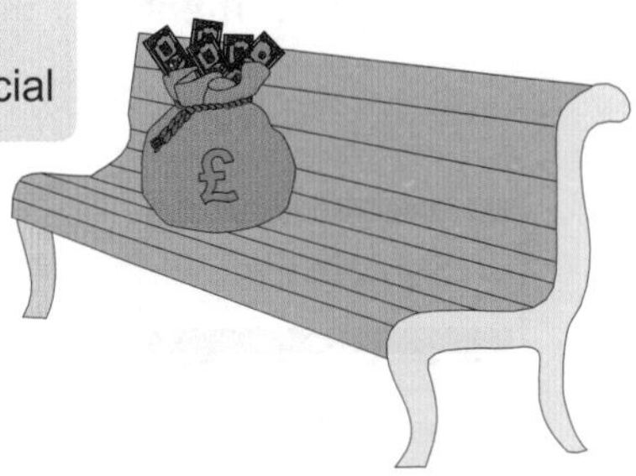

Alguien me ha robado el bolso. = Someone has stolen my bag.

my necklace:	el collar
my credit card:	la tarjeta de crédito

Someone's stolen my favourite paper clip...

Complaining and reporting crimes is quite fun if you get to do it in your speaking assessment — it's a bit more dramatic than just talking about the weather or something. And if you ever do get your bag stolen on holiday, at least you can impress the police with your knowledge of Spanish.

At a Restaurant

Going to a restaurant in Spain or Latin America is no end of fun...

¿Tiene una mesa libre? — Do you have a table free?

Don't forget — it's all about being polite.

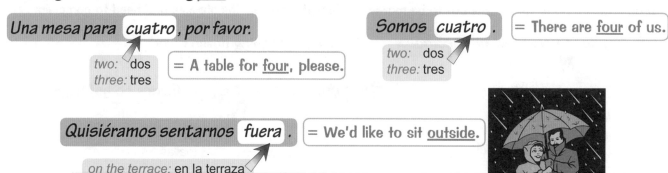

Una mesa para **cuatro***, por favor.* = A table for four, please.

two: dos
three: tres

Somos **cuatro***.* = There are four of us.

two: dos
three: tres

Quisiéramos sentarnos **fuera***.* = We'd like to sit outside.

on the terrace: en la terraza

You might see these signs in a restaurant

= Open

= Closed

= Opening hours: Monday to Saturday 7.30pm - 11pm

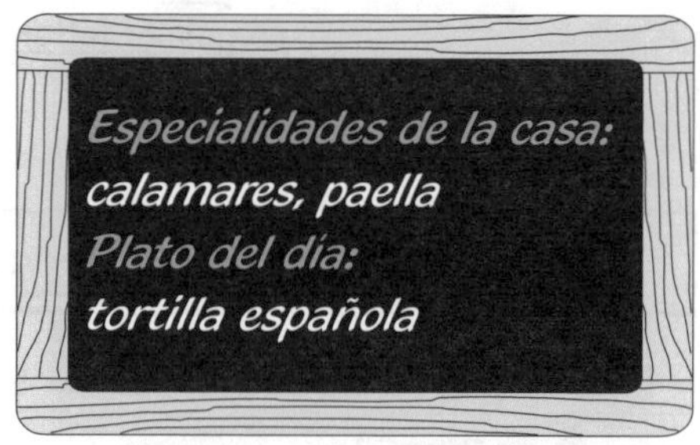

Especialidades de la casa:
calamares, paella
Plato del día:
tortilla española

= Specialities of the house: squid, paella
Dish of the day: Spanish omelette

= à la carte menu, fixed price menu

Reservado

= Reserved

= Please wait here

= No smoking

= Tips

= Toilets

Servicio incluido

= Service included

I'm sorry, this page is reserved...

I love restaurants — a chance to show off your language skills, order some exotic foods and be ill for weeks. Well, not that last one, maybe. You might have to recognise signs in your reading exam, so make sure you know them — especially the difference between 'servicio' and 'servicios'...

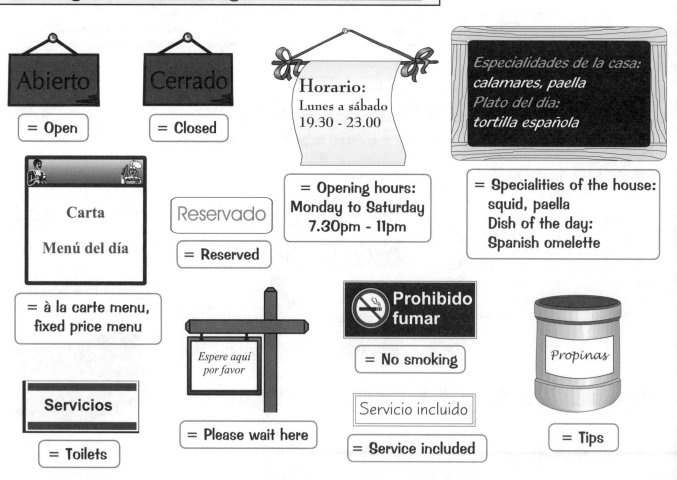

At a Restaurant

Phew — it's hungry work, all this talking about dinners and restaurants... Might be a good time to have a bar of chocolate or an apple... You wouldn't want your rumbling belly distracting you.

Quisiera... — I'd like...

¿Tiene paella? = Do you have paella?

bread: pan
bananas: plátanos

the omelette: la tortilla
the dish of the day: el plato del día

salad: ensalada
rice: arroz
carrots: zanahorias

Quisiera el filete con patatas fritas. = I'd like the steak with chips.

Para mí, una hamburguesa, por favor. = I'll have a burger, please.

Quisiera probar... — I'd like to try...

You'd never learn all the different types of food — there are squillions.
So here's a handy sentence for when you don't know what something tastes like.

¿A qué sabe el turrón? = What does turrón taste like?

rabbit: el conejo

No estoy satisfecho/a — I'm not satisfied

If you want to complain about something, remember to say what you're complaining about:

Quisiera quejarme. = I'd like to make a complaint.

La carne de ternera está poco hecha. = The veal is underdone.

The steak: El filete
The pork: La carne de cerdo
The coffee: El café

too hot: demasiado caliente
too cold: demasiado frío/a

¿Ha terminado? — Have you finished?

¿Puedo pagar? = Can I pay?

La cuenta, por favor. = The bill, please.

I want to complain — this gazpacho's cold...

Another 'must-learn' page, I'm afraid. Some of this stuff is useful in all sorts of situations — not just in a restaurant. There's a lot to remember — start by scribbling it down, covering and learning.

Talking About Your Holiday

Everyone wants to bore people by telling them all about their holidays. Yes, you too...
By the time you've finished this page you'll be able to bore people in Spanish... and get good marks.

¿Adónde fuiste? — Where did you go?

Fui a los Estados Unidos hace dos semanas. = I went to the USA two weeks ago.

to Spain: a España
to France: a Francia

a month ago: hace un mes
in July: en julio
in the summer: en el verano

¿Con quién fuiste? — Who did you go with?

Answer this question or there'll be all sorts of gossip.

Fui de vacaciones con mi familia por un mes. = I went on holiday with my family for a month.

my brother: mi hermano
my friends: mis amigos/as

a fortnight: quince días
a week: una semana

Hice un intercambio en España. = I went on an exchange to Spain.

Fui a Chile para visitar a mi amigo por correspondencia. = I went to Chile to visit my penfriend.

my cousins: mis primos
my grandparents: mis abuelos

¿Qué hiciste? — What did you do?

You need to be able to say what you did on holiday — learn it well.

Fui a la playa. = I went to the beach.

to the disco: a la discoteca
to a museum: a un museo

Me relajé. = I relaxed.

I enjoyed myself: Lo pasé muy bien
I played tennis: Jugué al tenis

This is a reflexive verb — see p. 104.

¿Cómo viajaste allí? — How did you get there?

Remember the little word 'allí', which means 'there' — it's a useful one (see page 89 for more on this).

Fuimos allí en coche. = We went there by car.

plane: avión *boat:* barco

For more types of transport, see p. 44.

I went to London — the beach was lovely...

You need to understand other people talking about their holidays and talk about your own holidays. Cover the page, scribble, look back etc. Keep going till you've learnt everything on the page.

Talking About Your Holiday

Details are what it's all about. So plough on and learn this stuff as well...

¿Cómo fue el viaje? — How was the trip?

You can never have too many opinions as far as Spanish GCSE is concerned.

¿Cómo fueron tus vacaciones? = How was your holiday?

Me gustaron. = I liked it.

Así así. = So-so.

No me gustaron. = I didn't like it.

¿Adónde te gustaría ir? — Where would you like to go?

Mi sueño es ir a Rusia. = My dream is to go to Russia.

Tengo muchas ganas de viajar a Cuba. = I really want to travel to Cuba.

Me gusta ir a lugares con mucha historia. = I like going to places with a lot of history.

a beach: playa
lots of shops: muchas tiendas

¿Adónde irás? — Where will you go?

You've got to be able to talk about the future — what you will be doing...

For more info about the future tense, see the grammar section — p. 98.

¿Adónde irás? = Where will you go?

Voy a ir a América dentro de dos semanas. = I'm going to go to America in two weeks.

¿Con quién irás de vacaciones? = Who will you go on holiday with?

Voy a ir de vacaciones con mi familia por un mes. = I'm going to go on holiday with my family for a month.

¿Cómo irás? = How will you get there?

Voy a ir en coche. = I'm going to go by car.

¿Qué harás? = What will you do?

Voy a ir a la playa. = I'm going to go to the beach.

My dream is to go to Milton Keynes...

More details = more marks. Simple. You can always make up a holiday you didn't have, or invent things you did, as long as you know the Spanish words for it. Smile — it could be worse. Just.

Weather

You may talk about the weather in your speaking assessment. Or you might have to listen to a weather forecast in your listening exam — or you might be in Spain planning a picnic...

¿Qué tiempo hace? — What's the weather like?

These short sentences are the ones you definitely can't do without — and they're easy.

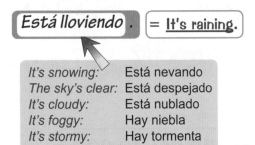

Está lloviendo. = It's raining.

It's snowing:	Está nevando
The sky's clear:	Está despejado
It's cloudy:	Está nublado
It's foggy:	Hay niebla
It's stormy:	Hay tormenta

Of course, it doesn't always rain, so here are a few others you could use:

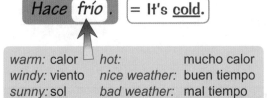

Hace frío. = It's cold.

warm:	calor	*hot:*	mucho calor
windy:	viento	*nice weather:*	buen tiempo
sunny:	sol	*bad weather:*	mal tiempo

¿Qué tiempo hará mañana? — What will the weather be like tomorrow?

This is quite easy, and it sounds dead impressive:

Mañana lloverá / va a llover. = It will rain tomorrow.

Next week:	La semana que viene
On Tuesday:	El martes

It'll snow:	nevará / va a nevar
It'll thunder:	habrá truenos
It'll be hot:	hará calor / va a hacer calor
It'll be cold:	hará frío / va a hacer frío
It'll be windy:	hará viento / va a hacer viento
It'll be cloudy:	estará nublado / va a estar nublado

Tomorrow it'll be wet.

See p. 2–3 for more on times and dates, and p. 98 for the future tense.

¿Qué tiempo hacía? — What was the weather like?

This is really handy for saying what the weather was like on holiday and that kind of thing.

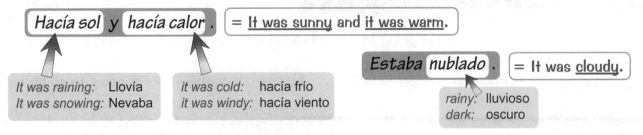

Hacía sol y hacía calor. = It was sunny and it was warm.

It was raining:	Llovía
It was snowing:	Nevaba

it was cold:	hacía frío
it was windy:	hacía viento

Estaba nublado. = It was cloudy.

rainy:	lluvioso
dark:	oscuro

It's raining, it's pouring...

This stuff on weather could come up in the exams — so you've got to do it. Still, all you need to do is learn the main sentences on this page and the bits of vocab — and you'll be working for the Met Office in no time. Or at least you'll get a good mark in your GCSE if you learn this stuff.

Revision Summary

Phew — I don't know about you but I think I need a holiday after all that. There's loads to learn in this section, and unfortunately you can't just absorb it all by touching the pages (I know — I've tried). So go over everything as many times as it takes, and then when you're ready have a go at these questions and see how well you've really remembered everything.

1) How do you say these countries in Spanish?
   a) England b) France c) Spain d) Germany e) USA f) Denmark g) Greece

2) Write down the names of four different regions of Spain, in English and Spanish.

3) Mrs Powell is taking her class on a school trip to Spain, and she wants to buy 18 second class return tickets to Madrid. What should she say?

4) You're at the train station and you want to know what time the train to Bilbao leaves. How would you ask this in Spanish?

5) Your Spanish penfriend Rosalía asks you "¿Te gusta viajar en tren?" What does the question mean, and how would you answer in Spanish?

6) Say in Spanish that you walk to school, but your friend goes on the bus.

7) You're in the tourist office in Barcelona. Ask for leaflets about excursions around Barcelona.

8) How would you ask in Spanish to change 200 pounds to euros?

9) What do these mean? a) las vacaciones b) la habitación individual c) la media pensión

10) You're booking a hotel in Spain. Ask for a single room with a balcony, and say that you want to stay for one week.

11) Once you've booked your room, the hotel receptionist tells you "Su habitación está en el cuarto piso, al final del pasillo. El desayuno se sirve a las ocho y media." What does this mean?

12) When you get to your room, you find that there are no towels and the television doesn't work. How would you tell the receptionist this in Spanish?

13) You've lost your passport. Tell the police in Spanish, and say that you lost it in the cathedral.

14) What do these signs mean? a) cerrado b) plato del día c) prohibido fumar d) propinas

15) You're in a restaurant with your friend Rocío. She says "Quisiera la tortilla con ensalada." What has she ordered? Say that you would like a burger with chips.

16) You're writing a letter to your penfriend Alicia. Tell her that you went on an exchange to Peru a month ago, you went to the beach and went to a museum, and you enjoyed yourself.

17) ¿Qué tiempo hace hoy? Answer in Spanish.

Names of Buildings

You need to know the names for buildings for all sorts of things — arranging to meet people, asking for directions and talking about your town for a start. Yes, it's a bit dull, but you absolutely <u>have</u> to learn them.

Learn all these edificios — buildings

These are the basic, bog-standard '<u>learn-them-or-else</u>' buildings.

the bank: el banco

the butcher's: la carnicería

the church: la iglesia

the theatre: el teatro

the railway station: la estación (de trenes)

the post office: Correos (masc.)

the baker's: la panadería

the cinema: el cine

the supermarket: el supermercado

the market: el mercado

the castle: el castillo

the library: la biblioteca

Otros edificios — Other buildings

OK, I'll come clean. There are absolutely <u>loads</u> of buildings you need to <u>know</u>. Like these:

MORE SHOPS

the shop:	la tienda
the chemist's:	la farmacia
the cake shop:	la pastelería
the newsagent, sweet shop:	el kiosco / quiosco
the department store:	los grandes almacenes
tobacconist's: (where you can buy stamps)	el estanco

TOURISTY BITS

the hotel:	el hotel
the youth hostel:	el albergue juvenil
the restaurant:	el restaurante
the tourist information office:	la oficina de turismo
the museum:	el museo
the zoo:	el zoo

OTHER IMPORTANT PLACES

the town hall:	el ayuntamiento
the cathedral:	la catedral
the park:	el parque
the airport:	el aeropuerto
the university:	la universidad
the swimming pool:	la piscina
the sports ground:	el campo deportivo
the bull ring:	la plaza de toros
the leisure centre:	el polideportivo
the stadium:	el estadio
the secondary school:	el instituto, el colegio
the primary school:	la escuela
the hospital:	el hospital

What about the candlestick maker's...

OK, so learning vocab's not the most exciting thing you could be doing right now. But you'll be a bit <u>stuck</u> when it comes to asking for <u>directions</u> if you don't know the word for the place you're trying to get to. So <u>turn over</u> the page and keep writing the words down till you've got them all.

Asking Directions

You might get at least one question about directions.
It's not too complicated — but it's worth getting straight in your mind now.

¿Dónde está... ? — Where is... ?

It's dead easy to ask where a place is — say '¿Dónde está...?' and stick the place on the end.

¿Dónde está la estación, por favor? = Where is the station, please?

¿Hay una biblioteca por aquí? = Is there a library near here?

See p. 56 for more buildings.

¿Está lejos de aquí? — Is it far from here?

If the place you're looking for is miles away, you don't just want to set off walking there.

¿Está el cine lejos de aquí? = Is the cinema far from here?

the tourist office:	la oficina de turismo
the park:	el parque
the museum:	el museo

Está a dos kilómetros. = It's two kilometres away.

a hundred metres away:	a cien metros
nearby:	cerca
far away:	lejos

Use '¿para ir a...?' to ask the way

Directions could easily come up in the listening exam, so you need to be able to understand them.

Por favor, señor, ¿para ir al banco? = Excuse me sir, how do I get to the bank?

(to a woman): señora

to the station:	a la estación
to the library:	a la biblioteca
to the castle:	al castillo

Important bit: Replace this with any place, using "al" for "el" words and "a la" for "la" words. See p. 89.

right at the traffic lights:	gire a la derecha en el cruce de los semáforos
straight on, past the church:	todo recto, pasando la iglesia
take the first road on the left:	tome / coja la primera a la izquierda

Look at p. 1 for more stuff on 1st, 2nd, etc.

You'll need all this vocab to understand directions.

go straight on:	siga todo recto / derecho
go right:	gire a la derecha
go left:	gire a la izquierda
on the corner:	en la esquina
just round the corner: (i.e. really near)	justo a la vuelta de la esquina

So, tell me again how to get to the library.

Is this the way to Amarillo...

Cover it up, scribble it down, check what you got wrong, and try it again. That's the way to learn this stuff. Keep at it until you know it all — then you'll be really ready for your exams. Just reading the page once isn't enough — you wouldn't remember it tomorrow, never mind in an exam.

Where You're From

You're a foreigner in Spain so you need to be able to say what country you're from and what your nationality is. It'll be handy to know some others too as they may well come up in your exams.

¿De dónde eres? — Where do you come from?

Some useful phrases here — and so easy to learn. There's no excuse to forget them, is there... If the country you're from isn't somewhere here, look it up in a dictionary.

Soy de Inglaterra. *Soy* inglés/inglesa. = I come from England. I am English.

Wales:	(del país) de Gales
Ireland:	de Irlanda
Northern Ireland:	de Irlanda del Norte
England:	de Inglaterra
Scotland:	de Escocia

Welsh:	galés/galesa
Northern Irish:	norirlandés/norirlandesa
English:	inglés/inglesa
Scottish:	escocés/escocesa
British:	británico/a

IMPORTANT BIT: When you're talking about girls you must drop the accent and add 'a' on the end of nationalities that end in 'és'.

¿Dónde vives? = Where do you live?

Vivo en Inglaterra. = I live in England.

Las nacionalidades — Nationalities

And now for a lovely list of nationalities. Any of these could come up in the reading or listening exams, so don't ignore them just because you don't know anyone from Portugal or Austria or wherever.

Irish	irlandés/irlandesa	*North American:*	norteamericano/a
European:	europeo/a	*South American:*	sudamericano/a
Spanish:	español/a	*Latin American:*	latinoamericano/a
French:	francés/francesa	*Mexican:*	mexicano/a
Italian:	italiano/a		mejicano/a
Portuguese:	portugués/portuguesa	*Argentinian:*	argentino/a
German:	alemán/alemana	*Peruvian:*	peruano/a
Austrian:	austríaco/a	*Chilean:*	chileno/a
Dutch:	holandés/holandesa	*Colombian:*	colombiano/a
American:	americano/a	*Cuban:*	cubano/a

For the countries to go with these nationalities, see p. 41.

IMPORTANT: Don't use a capital letter for inglés, francés etc.

¿Dónde vives? — Where do you live?

Vivo en Haxby. = I live in Haxby.

Haxby *está cerca de* York. = Haxby is near York.

Haxby *es un pueblo con* nueve mil *habitantes.* = Haxby is a town with 9000 inhabitants.

Haxby está en el noreste *de* Inglaterra. = Haxby's in the north-east of England.

the north:	el norte	*the south:*	el sur	*the south-east:*	el sureste
the east:	el este	*the west:*	el oeste	*the north-west:*	el noroeste

El paisaje alrededor de Haxby es muy bonito y verde. = The landscape around Haxby is very beautiful and green.

Isn't holandés the sauce you put on salmon...

All this stuff is really useful if you're meeting new people and you want to tell them where you're from and find out where they're from. Most of the nationalities are simple if you know the words for the countries in Spanish because they're similar — Alemania and alemán, Colombia and colombiano, etc.

Talking About Where You Live

Once you've said where you live, you need to be able to talk about what it's like there too.

En mi ciudad — In my town

This is another subject that comes up all the time — you need to understand what other people say about where they live, even if you don't have to talk about your own town.

¿Qué hay en tu ciudad? = What is there in your town?

small town / village: pueblo

Hay un mercado. = There's a market.

a cinema:	un cine
a park:	un parque
a shopping centre:	un centro comercial
a university:	una universidad

¿Cómo es Birmingham? — What's Birmingham like?

If you want a really good mark, make sure you're ready to give more details.

La ciudad es muy interesante. = The town is very interesting.

boring:	aburrida
great:	estupenda
dirty:	sucia
clean:	limpia
quiet / peaceful:	tranquila

Hay mucho que hacer. = There's lots to do.

There's not much:	No hay mucho
There's always something:	Siempre hay algo
There's nothing:	No hay nada

If you live in a village or small town it's 'el pueblo' so any adjectives you use with it will need to end in an 'o' not an 'a'.

¿Te gusta vivir en Birmingham? = Do you like living in Birmingham?

Me encanta vivir en Birmingham. = I love living in Birmingham.

I like:	Me gusta
I don't like:	No me gusta

Put them all together and make longer sentences — you'll get extra marks if you get it right.

Me gusta vivir en Birmingham porque siempre hay algo que hacer. = I like living in Birmingham because there's always something to do.

No me gusta vivir en Swampton porque no hay nada que hacer. = I don't like living in Swampton because there's nothing to do.

Imagine coming from a place called Swampton...

Seriously — who would call a town that? And yet there's one in Hampshire and another one in Kentucky. Chances are there's something to say about where you live, but if it's truly dull then make something up. See how much you can say about your town without looking at the page.

Talking About Where You Live

Describing things — I reckon that's what it's all about. The more info you give, the more marks you're gonna get for it. Stands to reason, really...

¿Cuál es tu dirección? — What's your address?

Vivo en la calle de Lime número cuarenta y cuatro, en Lancaster.

= I live at 44 Lime Street, in Lancaster.

Mi código postal es LA25 ONH.

= My postcode is LA25 ONH.

If you're saying your postcode out loud, you'll need to say all the numbers and letters in Spanish. See p. 1 for numbers and p. 17 for the alphabet.

En tu casa — At your home

Vivo en una casa. = I live in a house.

a flat: un piso, un apartamento

See p. 84 for where to put adjectives.

Vivo en una casa pequeña y nueva. = I live in a small, new house.

big:	grande	*old:*	vieja
pretty:	bonita	*cold:*	fría
green:	verde	*modern:*	moderna

Mi apartamento está cerca de un parque. = My flat is near a park.

My house: Mi casa

the town centre:	del centro de la ciudad
the motorway:	de la autopista
the shops:	de las tiendas
a shopping centre:	de un centro comercial
a bus stop:	de una parada de autobús
a train station:	de una estación de trenes

Me gustaría vivir más cerca del centro de la ciudad. = I would like to live nearer to the city centre.

nearer to the train station:	más cerca de la estación de trenes
in a bigger house:	en una casa más grande
in a house with a garden:	en una casa con jardín

Where do I live — at home, mostly...

Where you live is a great topic cos you don't have to find out any new information. All you've got to do is work out how to describe your home. Start by scribbling down this page and learning it.

Inside Your Home

Luckily you won't need to give a full house tour — you just need a few things to say about your home.

¿Cómo es tu casa? — What's your house like?

¿Cómo es la cocina? = What's the kitchen like?

the living room: el salón
the bathroom: el cuarto de baño
the dining room: el comedor
the bedroom: el dormitorio

La cocina es grande. = The kitchen is big.

small: pequeño/a
tiny: muy pequeño/a

Las paredes son azules. = The walls are blue.

¿Qué muebles hay en tu dormitorio? = What furniture is there in your bedroom?

En mi dormitorio hay una cama, dos sillas y una mesa pequeña. = In my bedroom there is a bed, two chairs and a small table.

armchair:	un sillón	chair:	una silla	wardrobe:	un armario
sofa:	un sofá	mirror:	un espejo	cupboard:	un armario
lamp:	una lámpara	bed:	una cama	curtains:	cortinas
table:	una mesa	double bed:	una cama de matrimonio	carpet / rug:	una alfombra
shelf:	un estante	wall:	una pared	fitted carpet:	una moqueta

Mi casa tiene un jardín. = My house has a garden.

My flat: Mi piso
Mi apartamento

Tenemos flores en nuestro jardín. = We have flowers in our garden.

a tree: un árbol
a lawn: césped

¿Tienes tu propio dormitorio? — Do you have your own room?

Tengo mi propio dormitorio. = I have my own room.

Comparto un dormitorio con mi hermano. = I share a room with my brother.

my sister: mi hermana

I love: Me encanta
I don't like: No me gusta

No me importa compartir un dormitorio. = I don't mind sharing a room.

Me gustaría tener mi propio dormitorio. = I'd like to have my own room.

I share a room with some mice...

This is all stuff that could come up in the exams. If the list of things in your room looks a bit scary, start off with just a few — but make sure you understand all the words if you read or hear them.

Celebrations

Ooh, birthdays and Christmas and Easter — this might be the most exciting page so far...

¿Qué celebras? — What do you celebrate?

*En Gran Bretaña celebramos **la Navidad** en **diciembre**.* = In Great Britain we celebrate Christmas in December.

Christmas Eve:	la Nochebuena
New Year:	el Año Nuevo
Hanukkah:	Januká

January:	enero
winter:	invierno

La Semana Santa tiene lugar en primavera. = Easter takes place in spring.

New Year's Eve:	La Nochevieja
Ramadan:	Ramadán

autumn:	otoño
May:	mayo

*Mi cumpleaños es el **diez** de **abril**.* = My birthday is on the tenth of April.

3rd:	tres
15th:	quince
27th:	veintisiete

February:	febrero
August:	agosto
November:	noviembre

For more dates and months, see p. 3.

¿Cómo festejas tu cumpleaños? — How do you celebrate your birthday?

*Festejo **mi cumpleaños** con **mi familia**.* = I celebrate my birthday with my family.

Christmas:	la Navidad
New Year's Eve:	la Nochevieja
Epiphany:	el Día de Reyes

my friends:	mis amigos
my boyfriend:	mi novio
my girlfriend:	mi novia

*Cuando cumpla **dieciocho** años, tendré una fiesta muy grande con todos mis amigos.*

16:	dieciséis

= When I turn 18, I will have a really big party with all my friends.

*En mi cumpleaños, recibo **regalos** de mis amigos.* = On my birthday, I get presents from my friends.

At Christmas:	En Navidad
At Easter:	En Semana Santa
On my saint's day:	En mi santo

cards:	tarjetas
chocolate eggs:	huevos de chocolate

*En Navidad, es tradicional **comer pavo**.* = At Christmas, it's traditional to eat turkey.

On New Year's Eve:	En Nochevieja

to sing carols:	cantar canciones de Navidad
to eat 12 grapes:	comer doce uvas

I like to celebrate with a nice bit of revision...

This is quite a nice little topic. You might get people talking about traditions in their country in the listening exam, or an article on it in the reading, so learning it all would probably be a wise move.

The Environment

The environment's one of those topics you either love or hate. Whether you think it's a chance to say what you think about something real and important, or you're bored silly with the whole thing, you've got to learn it.

El medio ambiente — ¿es importante para tí?

Is the environment important to you?

A question like this has to be answered with a yes, or a no, so remember to always listen out first for that in a listening exam... then try to figure out the reason.

No, no me interesa nada. = No, I'm not interested in it at all.

Sí, creo que el medio ambiente es muy importante. = Yes, I think the environment is very important.

Give opinions and arguments

If you're really up on 'green' matters then you could get well stuck into this, but if you're not then say so. You'll get as many marks for saying why you're not interested as you would for enthusing about Greenpeace.

Encontrar soluciones a los problemas medioambientales es la responsabilidad del gobierno.

= Finding solutions to the problems with the environment is the government's responsibility.

Me preocupa mucho el medio ambiente debido a la contaminación industrial.

= I'm really worried about the environment because of industrial pollution.

Las flores y la naturaleza son muy aburridas. Prefiero los juegos de ordenador.

= Flowers and nature are very boring. I prefer computer games.

Creo que la lluvia ácida provoca problemas muy graves.

pesticides: los pesticidas

= I think acid rain causes very serious problems.

ESSENTIAL ENVIRONMENT VOCAB

exhaust fumes:	los gases de escape	*air pollution:*	la contaminación del aire
pollution:	la contaminación	*natural resources:*	los recursos naturales
the greenhouse effect:	el efecto invernadero	*nature:*	la naturaleza
emissions:	las emisiones	*ozone layer:*	la capa de ozono
to damage:	dañar	*deforestation:*	la desforestación
to endanger:	poner en peligro	*global warming:*	el calentamiento global
extinction:	la extinción	*to blame:*	echar la culpa

I'm mad about the environment — I'm environ-mental...

There's quite a bit to learn here (especially that big horrible vocab list) but you can do it — just keep covering the page, writing down what you can remember and then checking it, like always.

The Environment

Here's how to show off about how environmentally-friendly you are, and talk about the future of the planet.

¿Qué haces para proteger el medio ambiente? — What do you do to protect the environment?

Reutilizo las bolsas de plástico. = I re-use plastic bags.

Apago las luces cuando dejo una habitación. = I turn off the lights when I leave a room.

the television: la televisión

Siempre compro productos ecológicos. = I always buy environmentally-friendly products.

No voy de vacaciones al extranjero porque los aviones producen muchas emisiones. = I don't go on holiday abroad because planes produce lots of emissions.

Reciclo periódicos. = I recycle newspapers.

magazines:	revistas	*plastic:*	plástico
bottles:	botellas	*paper:*	papel
tins:	latas	*cardboard:*	cartón

Voy al instituto a pie en vez de ir en coche. = I go to school on foot instead of going by car.

on the bus: en autobús

¿Qué crees que va a pasar en el futuro? — What do you think will happen in the future?

En el futuro espero que podamos resolver todos los problemas medioambientales. = In the future I hope that we can solve all the environmental problems.

This is the subjunctive. See p. 106.

Creo que vamos a agotar el petróleo. = I think we're going to run out of oil.

fossil fuels: los combustibles fósiles

El agujero en la capa de ozono será más grande. = The hole in the ozone layer will be bigger.

I recycle dog hair...

Yes, I collect it from the carpet and then knit it into scarves. Environmentally friendly and stylish. Anyway, this is the last page of the section so learn it well and then it's Revision Summary time.

Revision Summary

That was a nice section wasn't it? Short and sweet. There's nothing too tricky apart from the environment pages, but make sure you learn as much of the vocab as you can so that you'll be prepared for anything in the exams. If you can answer all these questions then you'll win the prize of a lifetime — the chance to move onto Section 6.

1) What are these buildings in English? a) la iglesia b) Correos c) el mercado
2) What are these buildings in Spanish? a) the bank b) the castle c) the library
3) Make a list of eight more buildings in English and Spanish.
4) You're in Spain and you want to go to the cinema. Ask a passer-by how to get there.
5) The passer-by gives you the following directions: "Siga todo recto, pasando la plaza de toros. Luego gire a la izquierda. El cine está en la esquina." What has she told you?
6) You make a new friend at the cinema. He asks you "¿De dónde eres?" What does the question mean, and how would you answer it in Spanish?
7) Think of eight nationalities and write them out in English and Spanish.
8) Write three sentences about where you live. (Don't forget you can make something up if you can't think of anything to say.)
9) Your penfriend Gabriela sends you this email about her home:
   Vivo en un apartamento. Es pequeño pero muy bonito y moderno.
   Está cerca de las tiendas. Me gusta mucho mi apartamento.
   What does the message mean?
10) Write two sentences in Spanish describing one of the rooms in your house.
11) Gabriela asks you "¿Tienes tu propio dormitorio?" Write a reply in Spanish.
12) ¿Cómo festejas tu cumpleaños? Write two sentences.
13) You read this sentence in an article about traditions in Spain:
    En Nochevieja es tradicional comer doce uvas a medianoche.
    What does the sentence mean?
14) Pablo and Nerea are discussing the environment. Pablo thinks that the environment is boring and not important. Nerea thinks that the greenhouse effect is a serious problem, and she's worried about pollution. Write out their conversation in Spanish.
15) What are these environment words in English?
    a) los gases de escape b) la naturaleza c) la capa de ozono d) la desforestación
16) Write out a list in Spanish of three things you do to help the environment.
    (It's fine if they're made up, as long as they make sense.)

School Subjects

School subjects — as if you don't get enough of that at school. This is really important stuff though.

¿Qué asignaturas estudias? — What subjects do you study?

Write out your timetable in Spanish and learn it all.

Estudio español. = I study Spanish.

You don't need the 'el' or 'la' when you're saying what you study.

LANGUAGES

French:	el francés
German:	el alemán
Spanish:	el español
Italian:	el italiano
English:	el inglés

ARTS AND CRAFTS

art:	el dibujo
music:	la música
drama:	el arte dramático
food technology:	la cocina

HUMANITIES

history:	la historia
geography:	la geografía
philosophy:	la filosofía
religious studies:	la religión
literature:	la literatura

NUMBERS AND STUFF

maths:	las matemáticas
IT:	la informática
business studies:	el comercio
economics:	las ciencias económicas

SCIENCES

science:	las ciencias
physics:	la física
chemistry:	la química
biology:	la biología

PHYSICAL EDUCATION

PE: la educación física

¿Cuál es tu asignatura favorita? — What's your favourite subject?

Or your least hated subject if that's how you feel about it all...

¿Cuál es tu asignatura favorita / preferida? = What's your favourite subject?

Mi asignatura preferida es el español. = My favourite subject is Spanish.

Prefiero la biología. = I prefer biology.

Me gustan las matemáticas. = I like maths.

I love:	Me encantan
I don't like:	No me gustan

There's more on how to say what you like and don't like on p. 7–8.

No me gusta nada la informática. = I don't like IT at all.

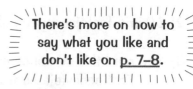

Odio la educación física. = I hate PE.

I'm subjected to school every day...

School subjects are bound to come up in your exams one way or another. Make sure you can say all the subjects you do, and at least understand the ones you don't do when you hear them.

School Routine

Not the most exciting of pages ever, but it's worth all the effort when you're talking about school routine. Go for short snappy sentences — that way they're easier to remember.

¿Cómo vas al instituto? — How do you get to school?

Voy al instituto en coche. = I go to school by car.

on foot:	a pie
by bus:	en autobús
by bike:	en bicicleta

Tardo veinte minutos en llegar al instituto. = It takes me twenty minutes to get to school.

Una clase — a lesson

Write out all these sentences and practise slotting in the right times and numbers for your school.

Las clases comienzan a las nueve. = School starts at 9 o'clock.

at twenty to nine:	a las nueve menos veinte
at half past eight:	a las ocho y media

For more on times, see p. 2.

Las clases terminan a las tres y cuarto. = School ends at quarter past 3.

Tenemos ocho clases por día. = We have 8 lessons per day.

Cada clase dura cuarenta minutos. = Each lesson lasts 40 minutes.

half an hour:	media hora
an hour:	una hora
an hour and a half:	una hora y media

El recreo es a las once. = Break is at 11 o'clock.

Lunch break: El descanso para almorzar

Hacemos una hora de deberes por día. = We do one hour of homework every day.

Una clase — let that be a lesson to you...

Don't forget the phrases for your exciting school routine, and the sentences for saying how you go to school. Remember the handy phrase 'por día' — you can stick it in loads of sentences.

School Routine

School is still about 99% of your life so it makes sense that you're going to be expected to read, write, talk or hear about it in Spanish.

¿Cómo es tu instituto? — What's your school like?

This is all a bit more tricky and also fairly random, but if you want a top mark, you need to learn it.

Tenemos seis semanas de vacaciones en el verano. = We have six weeks' holiday in the summer.

eight weeks: ocho semanas
five days: cinco días

at Christmas: en Navidad
at Easter: en Semana Santa

Hay tres trimestres. = There are three terms.

Las reglas son estrictas. = The rules are strict.

Los profesores nos dejan castigados si no hacemos los deberes. = The teachers put us in detention if we don't do our homework.

¿Tienes que llevar uniforme? — Do you have to wear a uniform?

Llevamos uniforme en el instituto. = We wear a uniform at school.

Nuestro uniforme es un jersey rojo, pantalones grises, una camisa blanca y una corbata verde. = Our uniform is a red jumper, grey trousers, a white shirt and a green tie.

Es optativo llevar uniforme. = Wearing a uniform is optional.

compulsory: obligatorio

See p. 35 for more on colours and p. 36 for clothes.

No me gusta llevar uniforme porque es muy feo. = I don't like wearing a uniform because it's really ugly.

No me importa llevar uniforme porque no tengo que decidir qué ponerme para ir al instituto. = I don't mind wearing a uniform because I don't have to decide what to wear to go to school.

School rules — not as far as I'm concerned...

You know all this stuff in English, so you're over the first hurdle already. It's just a case of learning how to say it all in Spanish. Close the book and see how much you can remember.

Classroom Language

We all have our 'off' days, so it's really useful to be able to ask someone to repeat something, or spell out a word you're not sure about. The stuff at the top of the page is useful, too.

¡Siéntate! — Sit down!

Learn these three short phrases to avoid the wrath of a scary teacher.

¡Levántate! = Stand up!

Stand up! (plural): ¡Levantaos!

¡Siéntate! = Sit down!

Sit down! (plural): ¡Sentaos!

¡Silencio! = Be quiet!

If you don't understand say "No entiendo"

These phrases can be vital in your speaking assessment. Even if the worst happens, it's far better to say 'I don't understand' in Spanish than to just shrug or say something in English.

¿Me puedes explicar esta palabra? = Can you (informal) explain this word?

Can you (formal): puede

(No) entiendo / comprendo. = I (don't) understand.

¿Qué quiere decir eso? = What does that mean?

No lo sé. = I don't know.

¿Puedes repetir eso, por favor? = Can you (informal) repeat that, please?

¿No es correcto? = Is that wrong?

No es correcto. = That's wrong.

Eso es. = That's right.

¿Cómo se dice en español? = How do you say that in Spanish?

En mi mochila — In my school bag

Here's a handy list of things you might find in your school bag.

a pen:	un bolígrafo / un boli	*scissors:*	unas tijeras
a pencil:	un lápiz	*a calculator:*	una calculadora
a rubber:	una goma	*a pencil case:*	un estuche
a ruler:	una regla	*a book:*	un libro
a pencil sharpener:	un sacapuntas	*an exercise book:*	un cuaderno
pencil crayons:	unos lápices de colores	*a dictionary:*	un diccionario

Mind your classroom language...

You can save yourself from an embarrassing silence in your speaking assessment if you learn these dead useful phrases. Just remember, bouts of forgetfulness happen to everyone so don't panic.

Problems at School

School isn't all fun and games, you know (is it ever...?). You need to know about school-related problems too.

El acoso escolar — Bullying

Bullying's not the cheeriest of topics, but it's best to know these phrases in case they come up.

El acoso escolar ***es un gran problema*** *en mi instituto.*

doesn't happen: no ocurre

= Bullying is a big problem at my school.

Los profesores ***no ayudan*** *a las víctimas del acoso escolar.*

(they) help: ayudan
(they) support: apoyan

= The teachers don't help victims of bullying.

Algunos estudiantes ***golpean*** *a otros.*

(they) insult: insultan
(they) intimidate: intimidan

= Some students hit others.

El estrés — Stress

Now's the chance to get all your school and exam woes off your chest.

Tengo muchos exámenes y no quiero suspenderlos.

= I have lots of exams and I don't want to fail them.

Si saco malas notas en los deberes, mis padres se enfadan conmigo.

= If I get bad marks for my homework, my parents get angry with me.

Si no apruebo los exámenes, no podré ***ir a la universidad****.*

be a doctor: ser médico/a
go on holiday: ir de vacaciones

= If I don't pass my exams, I won't be able to go to university.

Estoy muy estresado(/a) por los exámenes.

= I'm really stressed about my exams.

The best days of your life...

That was a bit of a depressing page, but don't just skip to something more pleasant — this stuff could come up in your exams, so you need to be prepared and learn as much of it as you can.

Work Experience

Everyone's got to do work experience at some time or another. Even if your time hasn't come yet, you could still have to listen to people rambling on about their placements in the listening exam, so pay attention.

¿Qué hiciste como experiencia laboral? — What did you do for work experience?

Como experiencia laboral, trabajé en una oficina. = For work experience I worked in an office.

a hospital: un hospital
a shop: una tienda

Trabajé allí durante una semana y media. = I worked there for a week and a half.

¿Cómo fue el trabajo? — How was the work?

More opinions wanted — own up, did you or did you not like it...?

El trabajo fue duro. = The work was hard.

difficult: difícil
interesting: interesante

Me sentí muy solo/sola. = I felt very lonely.

comfortable: cómodo/cómoda
at home: en casa
isolated: aislado/aislada

Mis compañeros de trabajo no eran simpáticos. = My work colleagues weren't friendly.

were very friendly: eran muy simpáticos
were interesting: eran interesantes

Tengo un trabajo a tiempo parcial — I have a part-time job

Make these easier by choosing easy jobs and simple values — if only the rest of life was like that.

Soy dependiente(/a). = I am a shop assistant.

Gano cinco libras por hora. = I earn £5 per hour.

£4.00 per hour: cuatro libras por hora
£15 per week: quince libras por semana

For work experience I did photocopying, mainly...

A friend of mine asked for a work experience placement with animals because she was thinking of becoming a vet, and she ended up getting sent to an abattoir for two weeks. Be warned.

Plans for the Future

As if you didn't have enough on your mind with all your exams and revision, those pesky exam boards want you to make your mind up about what you want to do in the future too — and say it in Spanish.

¿Qué quieres hacer después del instituto? — What do you want to do after school?

Quiero estudiar para el bachillerato y luego estudiar geografía en la universidad. = I want to do A levels and then study geography at university.

'El bachillerato' is the Spanish equivalent of A levels.

Quiero tomar un año libre. = I want to take a year out.

Quiero empezar a trabajar. = I want to start working.

Quiero hacer un aprendizaje. = I want to do an apprenticeship.

Quiero estudiar música porque quisiera ser músico/a. = I want to study music because I'd like to be a musician.

French: francés
maths: matemáticas

teacher: profesor/a
accountant: contable

¿En qué te gustaría trabajar? — What job would you like to do?

Me gustaría ser agente de viajes. = I would like to be a travel agent.

Give a short and simple reason for why you want to do a particular job.

Quisiera ser médico(/a), porque el trabajo sería interesante. = I would like to be a doctor, because the work would be interesting.

plumber: fontanero/a
chef: cocinero/a
dentist: dentista

fun: divertido
easy: fácil

En mi trabajo, quiero resolver problemas. = In my job I would like to solve problems.

meet new people: conocer a gente nueva
work with numbers: trabajar con números
help people: ayudar a la gente
earn a lot of money: ganar mucho dinero

After school I want to have my tea and watch Hollyoaks...

Valuable stuff. Saying what you want to do with your life is pretty essential. If the truth's too hard to say, then say something simpler. This is the kind of thing they just love to slip into listening and reading exams too, so don't skip it unless you're prepared to deal with the consequences...

Types of Job

There are more jobs here than you can shake a stick at — and any of them could pop up in your Spanish exams. The jobs you and your family do are extra important.

Muchos trabajos — Lots of jobs

You'll need to be able to say and write any of the jobs you and your family do — and recognise the rest when you see or hear them.

OUTDOOR JOBS

mechanic:	el/la mecánico/a
electrician:	el/la electricista
plumber:	el/la fontanero/a
builder:	el/la albañil
labourer:	el/la obrero/a
carpenter:	el/la carpintero/a
farmer:	el/la granjero/a
gardener:	el/la jardinero/a
soldier:	el/la militar
firefighter:	el/la bombero/a
policeman/woman:	el/la policía
postman/woman:	el/la cartero/a
lorry driver:	el/la camionero/a

solicitor's office
I've been soliciting for 20 years now, and it hasn't got me anywhere.

ARTY JOBS

actor/actress:	el actor, la actriz
musician:	el/la músico/a
model:	el/la modelo
writer:	el/la escritor/a
painter:	el/la pintor/a

MEDICAL JOBS

dentist:	el/la dentista
chemist:	el/la farmacéutico/a
nurse:	el/la enfermero/a
doctor:	el/la médico/a
vet:	el/la veterinario/a

OFFICE JOBS

accountant:	el/la contable
engineer:	el/la ingeniero/a
executive:	el/la ejecutivo/a
lawyer/solicitor:	el/la abogado/a
businessman:	el hombre de negocios
businesswoman:	la mujer de negocios
receptionist:	el/la recepcionista
secretary:	el/la secretario/a
journalist:	el/la periodista
estate agent:	el/la agente inmobiliario/a
interpreter:	el/la intérprete
translator:	el/la traductor/a

A LOAD MORE JOBS

teacher:	el/la profesor/a
hairdresser:	el/la peluquero/a
flight attendant (female):	la azafata
flight attendant (male):	el auxiliar de vuelo
chef:	el/la cocinero/a
waiter/waitress:	el/la camarero/a
shopkeeper:	el/la comerciante
shop assistant:	el/la dependiente/a
baker:	el/la panadero/a
butcher:	el/la carnicero/a

ALTERNATIVES

student:	el/la estudiante
part-time worker:	el/la trabajador/a a tiempo parcial
apprentice:	el/la aprendiz
housewife:	el ama de casa

Female versions of jobs can be tricky

There are rules to how the female version of a job is formed, but there are also exceptions to every rule. The only way to be sure you get the female version right is to learn it.

MASCULINE/FEMININE

el ingeniero → *la ingeniera*		(an 'o' ending becomes 'a')
el pintor → *la pintora*		('or' becomes 'ora')
el contable → *la contable*		('e' just stays the same)

Watch out for words like modelo, dentista and recepcionista — the endings of these words don't change depending on the gender.

I used to know two Spanish firemen — José and Hose B...

None too nice, but start with the jobs you find the easiest — then learn the rest. Female versions of each job need learning, so don't forget those tricky odd ones. There's no proper word for 'househusband' in Spanish yet either — Spanish vocab hasn't quite caught up with feminism...

Pros and Cons of Different Jobs

You might need to say what you think are the good and bad points of different jobs. It's simple enough, as long as nobody asks you about the good points of being a sewer cleaner or something...

¿Cuáles son las ventajas de ser profesor? — What are the advantages of being a teacher?

*Una de las ventajas de ser **profesor** es que **las vacaciones son muy largas**.*

= One of the advantages of being a teacher is that the holidays are very long.

doctor:	médico/a
flight attendant:	azafata (female)
	auxiliar de vuelo (male)
gardener:	jardinero/a

they earn a lot of money:	ganan mucho dinero
they travel all over the world:	viajan por todo el mundo
they stay fit:	se mantienen en forma

*Lo mejor de ser **veterinario** es **trabajar con animales**.*

= The best thing about being a vet is working with animals.

hairdresser:	peluquero/a
interpreter:	intérprete

'Lo' plus an adjective means 'the ... thing/bit', e.g. 'lo interesante' means 'the interesting thing'. See p. 84 for more on this.

chatting to customers:	charlar con los clientes
meeting foreign people:	conocer a gente extranjera

¿Y las desventajas? — What about the disadvantages?

*Una de las desventajas de ser **profesor** es que **es un trabajo estresante**.*

= One of the disadvantages of being a teacher is that it's a stressful job.

*Lo peor de ser **cartero** es **tener que levantarse muy temprano**.*

= The worst thing about being a postman is having to get up very early.

Me gustaría ser bombero porque quiero ayudar a la gente, pero es un trabajo muy peligroso.

= I'd like to be a firefighter because I want to help people, but it's a very dangerous job.

Me gustaría ser camarero porque me gusta conocer a gente nueva, pero los camareros no ganan mucho dinero.

= I'd like to be a waiter because I like meeting new people, but waiters don't earn a lot of money.

Being a prison warden involves a lot of cons...

There's quite a lot of thinking involved in this page, but giving opinions and reasons for them will get you loads of marks. Advantages and disadvantages vocab is handy for all sorts of things too.

Working Abroad

Gap years are all the rage now, so you need to know how to talk about them in Spanish.

¿Te gustaría trabajar en el extranjero? — Would you like to work abroad?

Me gustaría hacer una práctica en España. = I'd like to do a work placement in Spain.

study at university: estudiar en la universidad

Después de hacer el bachillerato, me gustaría tomar un año libre en Méjico.

= After doing my A levels, I'd like to take a gap year in Mexico.

Este verano voy a trabajar en una oficina de turismo en Burgos.

an ice-cream parlour: una heladería
a baker's: una panadería

= This summer I'm going to work in a tourist office in Burgos.

Tomé un año libre en España — I took a gap year in Spain

Trabajé en un museo en Barcelona durante nueve meses. = I worked in a museum in Barcelona for nine months.

a souvenir shop: una tienda de recuerdos
a hotel: un hotel

six months: seis meses
a year: un año

Lo pasé muy bien. = I had a really good time.

good: bien
dreadful: fatal

Creo que mi español ha mejorado mucho. = I think my Spanish has improved a lot.

El trabajo era aburrido, pero mis compañeros eran muy amables.

difficult: difícil

= The work was boring, but my colleagues were very friendly.

No me pagaron, así que no podía viajar por España. = They didn't pay me, so I couldn't travel around Spain.

go out with my friends: salir con mis amigos
go shopping: ir de compras

I'd take a gap year, but I'm afraid of falling...

This is another pretty challenging page, but these pages are perfect if you're talking about your future plans or past experiences abroad in your writing or speaking assessment.

Getting a Job

The first step to finding a job is understanding the job advert.
Then you've just got to convince someone to employ you...

Ofertas de empleo — Job Vacancies

Buscamos un camarero/una camarera con un mínimo de un año de experiencia, para trabajar en un restaurante chino en Marbella, seis tardes por semana. Salario 7€ por hora. Llámanos al 665443221.

= We're looking for a waiter/waitress with a minimum of one year's experience to work in a Chinese restaurant in Marbella, six evenings a week. Wages 7€/hour. Call us on 665443221.

Se busca recepcionista de hotel que hable inglés y español. Experiencia necesaria. Solicitudes por correo electrónico: empleos@hotelxyz.es.

= Wanted: hotel receptionist who speaks English and Spanish. Experience necessary. Applications by email: empleos@hotelxyz.es.

Estoy buscando trabajo — I'm looking for a job

Estoy buscando trabajo en una oficina de turismo. = I'm looking for a job in a tourist information office.

a cinema: un cine

Tengo un año de experiencia como camarero. = I've got one year of experience as a waiter.

waitress: camarera
shop assistant: dependiente/a

Hablo español. = I speak Spanish.

Soy una persona trabajadora y cortés. = I am a hard-working and polite person.

honest: honrada
well-mannered: bien educada

¿Por qué quiere usted este trabajo? — Why do you want this job?

Business: El comercio

El turismo me interesa mucho. = Tourism interests me a lot.

Quisiera mejorar mi español. = I'd like to improve my Spanish.

animals: animales

Me gusta trabajar con niños. = I like working with children.

Wanted: time lord. Must have own time machine...

Learn all this and you'll be well on your way to becoming a high-flying executive in Spain.

Getting a Job

A lot of the stuff in your GCSEs uses the informal 'tú' form but for job applications you'll need to be super-polite and use the 'usted' form.

Una carta de solicitud — A letter of application

Sra. Guerrero,
C/ Goya, 123,
28030 Madrid

Hannah Osborne,
12 Crabtree Lane,
Cambridge CB5 0NH

Cambridge, el 12 de mayo de 2009

Estimada señora Guerrero:

Ayer leí su anuncio de trabajo en el periódico, y quisiera solicitar el puesto de Agente Inmobiliaria.

Creo que sería la candidata ideal porque tengo dos años de experiencia en ventas, y hablo inglés y español. Me gustaría trabajar como agente inmobiliaria porque me gusta conocer a gente nueva y me interesan las casas. Además, soy muy trabajadora y bien educada.

Adjunto una copia de mi curriculum.

Le saluda atentamente,

Hannah Osborne

Yesterday I read your job advertisement in the newspaper, and I would like to apply for the position of Estate Agent.

I think that I would be the ideal candidate because I have two years of experience in sales, and I speak English and Spanish. I would like to work as an estate agent because I like meeting new people, and I am interested in houses. Also, I am very hard-working and well-mannered.

I attach a copy of my C.V.

Un curriculum — A C.V.

CURRICULUM

Hannah Osborne

12 Crabtree Lane, Cambridge CB5 0NH
Teléfono: 02 02 24 25 36

EDUCACIÓN

2007: Licenciatura en Español

2002: A levels (equivalentes al bachillerato)
Español (A), Historia (B), Comercio (B)

EXPERIENCIA LABORAL

Desde 2007: Directora de Ventas, 'Soap by Sue', Cambridge.

2002-2003: Dependienta, 'Supermoda', Barcelona.

MÁS INFORMACIÓN

Idiomas: inglés, español
Carnet de conducir

EDUCATION

2007: Spanish degree

2002: A levels (equivalent to *bachillerato*)
Spanish (A), History (B), Business Studies (B)

WORK EXPERIENCE

Since 2007: Sales Director, 'Soap by Sue', Cambridge.

2002-2003: Sales Assistant, 'Supermoda', Barcelona.

FURTHER INFORMATION

Languages: English, Spanish
Driving licence

I'd be ideal because I'm a perfecshonist...

Most of this stuff isn't new, but get used to dealing with it in this context. So if one of the speaking tasks is about pretending you're applying for a job as a barber in Seville, it won't throw you.

Telephones

You could quite easily get a phone call to listen to in your listening exam.
If you learn this stuff and practise using it now, it could come in pretty handy.

Una llamada telefónica — A phone call

¿Cuál es tu número de teléfono? = What's your telephone number?

If you need to be more formal, use su.

Mi número de teléfono es el veintiocho, diecinueve, cincuenta y seis. = My telephone number is 281956.

Put your phone number in groups of 2, i.e. twenty-eight rather than two eight.

Answering the phone

Here are a few phrases that you might hear in phone calls.

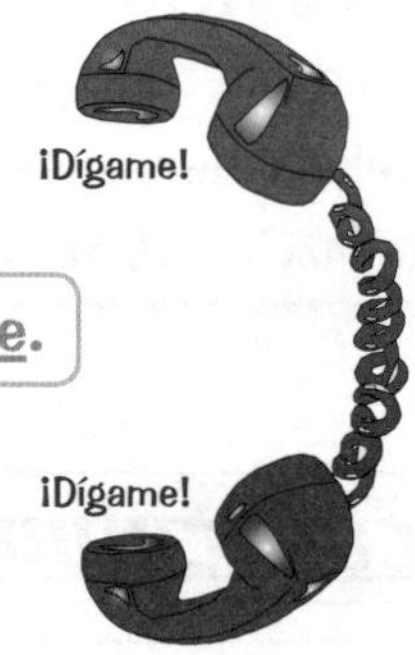

This is how you answer the phone: *¡Dígame!* = Hello?

And here's how to say who you are: *Hola, soy Louise.* = Hello, it's Louise.

¿Puedo hablar con Laura? = Can I speak to Laura?

¿Está Laura? = Is Laura there?

These two little gems both mean 'on the line' or 'speaking': *Hablando.* = Speaking. *Al aparato.* = Speaking.

¿Puede Laura llamarme a las siete? = Could Laura ring me back at seven?

Quisiera dejar un mensaje — I'd like to leave a message

Leaving a message is pretty similar to making a phone call — except that there's nobody at the other end.

Este mensaje es para Claudio. = This message is for Claudio.

Hola, soy Paula. Mi número de teléfono es el cincuenta y nueve, dieciocho, cuarenta y siete. ¿Puede llamarme Claudio a las ocho? Gracias. Hasta luego.

= Hello, it's Paula. My telephone number is 591847. Could Claudio ring me back at 8 o'clock? Thank you. Bye.

Phoning is my vocation — I felt called to it...

Time to cover up the page and write down the key phrases. Then, yep, it's learn and practise.

The Business World

The Spanish fun doesn't end once you've got a job — it goes on and on and on...

¿Le interesa comprar un bolso? — Are you interested in buying a handbag?

These little phrases could be really useful for your exams — and also if you ever go on the Spanish version of The Apprentice.

¿Le interesa comprar un microondas? = Are you interested in buying a microwave?

some gloves: unos guantes
a wardrobe: un armario

Son de muy alta calidad. = They're very high quality.

Vienen en cinco colores y en dos tamaños. = They come in five colours and two sizes.

El precio es muy razonable. = The price is very reasonable.

Hay un problema con mi pedido — There's a problem with my order

If you've got an unhappy customer, it's always good if you can understand what it is they're so annoyed about.

Pedí un ordenador portátil hace tres semanas y todavía no ha llegado. = I ordered a laptop three weeks ago and it still hasn't arrived.

Ustedes me han cobrado demasiado. = You've charged me too much.

Me han enviado el color equivocado. Pedí un jersey azul, pero el jersey que he recibido es marrón. = You've sent me the wrong colour. I ordered a blue jumper, but the jumper that I've received is brown.

Pedí dos bolsos y un paraguas, y falta el paraguas. = I ordered two handbags and an umbrella, and the umbrella is missing.

Lo siento. Arreglaré el problema tan pronto como pueda. = I'm sorry. I will sort out the problem as soon as I can.

Learn this page — and that's an order...

Don't forget that absolutely anything could come up in your reading and listening exam, and that includes this little lot. The problem phrases are useful for letters of complaint too (see p. 11).

Revision Summary

That's the end of another section. And that means that you're just one section away from the end of the book. Don't get too excited though because it's the grammar section. Make sure you can answer all these questions without looking back at the pages, and then it's grammar time.

1) Say what all your GCSE subjects are in Spanish (or as many as possible).

2) Your friend Ana asks you "¿Cuál es tu asignatura preferida?"
What does the question mean, and how would you reply in Spanish?

3) How would you say that your lunch break is at 12.45 and that it lasts an hour?

4) Sukia has to wear a uniform at school, but she doesn't like it because it's ugly. Her uniform is a yellow skirt, a green shirt and a pink tie. How would she say all this in Spanish?

5) What do these classroom phrases mean?
a) ¡Siéntate! b) No entiendo c) No lo sé d) ¿Puedes repetir eso, por favor?

6) ¿Estás estresado/a por los exámenes? ¿Y por qué? Answer in Spanish.

7) Your friend Noelia is telling you about her work experience placement: "Como experiencia laboral, trabajé en un hospital durante quince días. El trabajo fue interesante y mis compañeros de trabajo eran simpáticos." What does this mean?

8) Write three sentences in Spanish about your plans for the future. (If you're not sure what you want to do in the future, just invent something believable.)

9) A Carlos le gustaría ser cocinero porque le gusta la comida y cree que el trabajo sería divertido. ¿Cómo se dice esto en inglés?

10) What are these jobs in English?
a) el camionero b) el veterinario c) el periodista d) el carnicero e) el fontanero

11) Choose any job (that you know the name for in Spanish) and write down one advantage and one disadvantage of that job.

12) Write down in Spanish that you'd like to do a work placement in Spain after doing your A levels.

13) You see this job advert in a newspaper:
Se busca un/a enfermero/a con un mínimo de dos años de experiencia.
Tiempo parcial. Salario 700€ por mes. Solicitudes por correo electrónico.
What does the advert mean?

14) You are doing work experience for a mail-order sock company in Bilbao. One morning when you arrive in the office, this message is on the answer machine:
"Hola, soy Faviola Conuve. Pedí unos calcetines rojos, pero los calcetines que he recibido son verdes. ¿Puede llamarme alguien a las once de la mañana? Mi número de teléfono es cuarenta y seis, veintidós, diecisiete. Gracias. Adiós."
Write out the message in English.

Words for People and Objects

Nouns

Stop — before you panic, this stuff is a lot less scary than it looks.
It's all pretty simple stuff about words for people and objects — nouns. This is really important.

Every Spanish noun is masculine or feminine

Whether a word is masculine, feminine or plural affects a lot of things. All 'the' and 'a' words change, and as if that weren't enough, the adjectives (like big, red, shiny) change to fit the word.

Examples

a small dog: un perro pequeño *(masculine)*
a small house: una casa pequeña *(feminine)*

For more on this, see p. 82 and 83.

It's no good just knowing the Spanish words for things, you have to know whether each one's masculine or feminine too.

THE GOLDEN RULE
Each time you learn a word, remember the el or la to go with it — don't think 'dog = perro', think 'dog = el perro'.

EL, LA, LOS AND LAS
An el in front usually means it's masculine.
La in front = feminine.

These rules help you guess what a word is

Rules of Thumb for Masculine and Feminine Nouns

MASCULINE NOUNS:	FEMININE NOUNS:
most nouns that end:	most nouns that end:
-o -l -n -r -s	-a ción -sión -tad
-ma -pa -ta -aje	-tud -dad -umbre
also: male people, languages, days, months, seas, rivers, oceans, and mountains.	also: female people, letters of the alphabet.

You can't tell whether a noun ending in 'e' or 'ista' is masculine or feminine, e.g.

the car:	el coche
the people:	la gente
the tourist (man):	el turista
the tourist (woman):	la turista

Making Nouns Plural

1) Nouns in Spanish are usually made plural by adding an 's' when they end in a vowel and 'es' when they end in a consonant.

   e.g. one orange: una naranja
   two oranges: dos naranjas

2) Family surnames and nouns which finish in an unstressed syllable ending in 's' stay the same in the plural.

   e.g. the Simpsons (family): Los Simpson
   e.g. Tuesday: el martes *Tuesdays:* los martes

3) You may need to add or remove an accent when nouns become plural to keep the pronunciation.

   e.g. one young man: un joven
   two young men: dos jóvenes
   e.g. one Englishman: un inglés
   two Englishmen: dos ingleses

4) Nouns ending in 'z' change the 'z' to a 'c' before adding 'es'.

   e.g. one pencil: un lápiz *two pencils:* dos lápices

5) When you make a masculine noun plural, instead of 'el' you have to use 'los' to say 'the'. For feminine nouns 'la' becomes 'las' when it's plural — see p. 82.

TOP TIP FOR PLURALS
Each time you learn a word, learn how to make it into a plural too.

Masculine words — butch, hunky, stud...

The bottom line is — every time you learn a word in Spanish, you have to learn whether it's el or la, and you have to learn what its plural is. So start as you mean to go on — get into genders.

ARTICLES

'The' and 'A'

'The' and 'a' are a bit tricky in Spanish, because they're different for masculine, feminine or plural words.

'The' — el, la, los, las

1) Spanish 'the' changes for masculine, feminine or plural:

Masculine singular:	**el**	e.g. el chico (the boy)	Masculine plural:	**los**	e.g. los chicos (the boys)
Feminine singular:	**la**	e.g. la chica (the girl)	Feminine plural:	**las**	e.g. las chicas (the girls)

2) But remember 'el' is used before feminine nouns which start with a stressed 'a': *e.g. The water is cold.* El agua está fría.

3) You can't say 'a el', 'de el', so you say 'al' (a + el) and 'del' (de + el) instead.
e.g. I went to the park. Fui al parque. *e.g. He's the president's son.* Es el hijo del presidente.

'El', 'la', 'los' and 'las' are definite articles.

4) Sometimes you need a definite article in Spanish when you wouldn't use one in English.
   a) with nouns used in a general sense: *e.g. I don't like coffee.* No me gusta el café.
   b) in front of days of the week and times: *e.g. Every Monday at five o'clock.* Todos los lunes a las cinco.
   c) in front of weights and measurements: *e.g. 2 euros a kilo.* Dos euros el kilo.
   d) when you talk about a person and give their title: *e.g. How is Mr Jiménez?* ¿Cómo está el señor Jiménez?

5) There's also a neuter article 'lo' for things that aren't masculine or feminine. You'll mostly come across it in phrases: Lo mejor/peor: *the best/worst thing* Lo que: *what/that which* No sé lo que quiere: *I don't know what he wants.*

'A' — un, una

Masculine: **un** e.g. tengo un hermano (I have a brother) Feminine: **una** e.g. tengo una hermana (I have a sister)

1) 'A' is left out: a) after the verb 'ser' when talking about someone's occupation or nationality: *e.g. I'm a student*: Soy estudiante
   b) after a negative word: *e.g. I haven't got a cat.* No tengo gato.
   c) in front of 'otro/a': *e.g. Do you want another coffee?* ¿Quieres otro café?

'Un' and 'una' are indefinite articles.

2) When you make 'un' or 'una' plural, they mean 'some' or 'a few'. *I spent a few days at the beach.* Pasé unos días en la playa. *I have some very good photos.* Tengo unas fotos muy buenas.

Any, each, all and another

1) Here's something worth knowing — you don't need a special word for 'any': *Have you got any apples?* ¿Tienes manzanas? *Juan doesn't want any bread.* Juan no quiere pan.

2) Use 'otro' or 'otra' for 'another' — remember it's not 'un otro' or 'una otra'. *I'll do it another day.* Lo haré otro día. *I wrote another letter.* Escribí otra carta.

3) 'All' is 'todo/toda/todos/todas'. *He studies all day.* Estudia todo el día. *I bought all the books.* Compré todos los libros.

4) Use 'cada' to say 'each' — it stays the same for masculine and feminine words, and you can only use it with singular words. *Each dress has a unique design.* Cada vestido tiene un diseño único.

La la la la, I'm not listening...

Blimey, am I glad I speak English — just one word for 'the', and no genders. This stuff might be dull but it's important — you won't get very far with Spanish unless you get to grips with genders.

Words to Describe Things

ADJECTIVES

Gain more marks and show what an interesting person you are by using some juicy describing words. Make sure you understand what you're saying as well.

Adjectives must 'agree' with the thing they're describing

1) In English, you can use the same describing word (adjective) for whatever you like — like tall sunflower, tall sunflowers, tall man, tall woman, tall women...
2) In Spanish, the describing word has to change to match whether what it's describing is masculine or feminine, singular or plural. Even if the adjective isn't next to the word it's describing in the sentence, it still needs to agree. Look at these examples where 'pequeño' has to change:

Masculine Singular	*Masculine Plural*	*Feminine Singular*	*Feminine Plural*
el chico pequeño	los chicos pequeños	la chica pequeña	las chicas pequeñas
(the small boy)	*(the small boys)*	*(the small girl)*	*(the small girls)*

"You stink!" "I agree."

1. When you look an adjective up in the dictionary it's listed in the masculine singular form. If the word being described is feminine (see p. 81), change the 'o' at the end of the adjective to an 'a'.

2. Add an '-s' or an '-es' to the describing word if the word being described is plural (see p. 81). If it's feminine plural, it'll end up with '-as' on the end.

3) Some colours never change at all, because they are actually the names of things, and are not real adjectives. The most common ones are:

beige:	beige	*pink:*	rosa
cream:	crema	*turquoise:*	turquesa
orange:	naranja	*violet:*	violeta

e.g. Three orange hats.
Tres sombreros naranja.

See p. 35 for more colours.

Some handy describing words

Here are some really important describing words — they're the ones you really have to know.

SIZE WORDS

big:	grande
small:	pequeño/a
tall:	alto/a
short:	bajo/a
long:	largo/a
fat:	gordo/a
thin:	delgado/a

POSITIVE WORDS

good:	bueno/a
happy:	feliz
nice (character):	simpático/a
pretty/nice:	bonito/a
handsome/pretty:	guapo/a
interesting:	interesante
easy:	fácil

NEGATIVE WORDS

bad:	malo/a
sad:	triste
boring:	aburrido/a
strange:	raro/a
difficult:	difícil

A FEW MORE WORDS

old:	viejo/a
young:	joven
new:	nuevo/a
fast:	rápido/a
slow:	lento/a

Mi vecino es simpático.
= My neighbour is nice.

Tengo una bicicleta nueva.
= I have a new bike.

Las flores son bonitas.
= The flowers are pretty.

Compré unos libros interesantes.
= I bought some interesting books.

This page is interesting, don't you agree...

Aaaargh — more tables to learn, but then that's the nature of Spanish grammar. For these endings to be of any use to you, you need to learn the genders of the nouns in the first place. You have to know what your adjective needs to agree with. To get it right — get learning.

ADJECTIVES

Words to Describe Things

Once you've learned some describing words, you need to know where to put them.

Most describing words go after the word they describe

It's the opposite of English — in Spanish most describing words (adjectives) go after the word they're describing (the noun).

Es un vestido horrible. = It's a horrible dress.

Occasionally you might see some adjectives before the word they describe, but it's not very common:

No voy a comprar ese horrible vestido. = I'm not going to buy that horrible dress.

Some describing words always go in front of the word they're describing. These are the most common ones:

each, every:	cada	*other:*	otros/as	*so many:*	tantos/as
a lot of:	mucho/a	*little (not much):*	poco/a	*first, second...:*	primero/a, segundo/a...
lots of:	muchos/as	*few:*	pocos/as		
another:	otro/a	*so much:*	tanto/a		

See p. 1 for more numbers.

Some adjectives change if they're before masculine nouns

1) Some adjectives lose the final 'o' when they go in front of a masculine noun:

good:	bueno/a	*some:*	alguno/a
first:	primero/a	*none:*	ninguno/a
third:	tercero/a	*bad:*	malo/a

Un buen día. = A good day.

2) 'Alguno' and 'ninguno' both drop an 'o' and add an accent:

No hay ningún taxi libre. = There's no taxi free.

3) 'Grande' is the only adjective that drops 'de' in front of both masculine and feminine words.

Una gran señora. = A great lady.

4) 'Ciento' drops 'to' when it comes in front of anything that isn't another number (except 'mil' or 'millón').

Cien euros. = One hundred euros.

Some change their meaning depending on their position

Some adjectives change their meaning according to whether they are before or after the noun. Here are some important ones — learn them carefully.

adjective	meaning if it's before the noun		meaning if it's after the noun	
grande	great	un gran hombre (a great man)	big	un hombre grande (a big man)
mismo	same	el mismo día (the same day)	self	yo mismo (I myself)
nuevo	new (different)	tengo un nuevo coche (I have a new [to me] car)	(brand) new	tengo un coche nuevo (I have a brand new car)
viejo	old (longstanding)	un viejo amigo (an old friend)	old (elderly)	un amigo viejo (an elderly friend)

Add 'ito' or 'ísimo' to make adjectives smaller or stronger

You can add 'ito/a' to almost any adjective to make things seem smaller or cuter, or 'ísimo/a' to make the meaning stronger.

El bebé está enfermito. = The baby is poorly.

La película es malísima. = The film is really awful.

Use 'lo' with an adjective to mean 'the ... thing'

You can use 'lo' and any masculine adjective to mean 'the good/bad/best/worst/interesting/funny... thing'.

Lo malo de la película es que es muy larga. = The bad thing about the film is that it's very long.

Can adding 'ísimo' make people stronger...

It'd be a lot simpler than all that weightlifting. This page isn't too taxing — make sure you're clear on which adjectives go where, and don't get tripped up by the ones that change their meaning.

Words to Describe Things

ADJECTIVES

Ooh — a lovely page all about belonging words. Cool.

My, your, our — who things belong to

You have to be able to use and understand these words to say that something belongs to someone:

You have to choose masculine, feminine, singular or plural to match the thing it's describing, not the owner.

Mi hermano es alto. = My brother is tall.

Tus zapatos son bonitos. = Your shoes are nice.

	masculine singular	feminine singular	masculine plural	feminine plural
my	mi	mi	mis	mis
(singular familiar) your	tu	tu	tus	tus
his/her/its/(singular polite) your	su	su	sus	sus
our	nuestro	nuestra	nuestros	nuestras
(plural familiar) your	vuestro	vuestra	vuestros	vuestras
their/(plural polite) your	su	su	sus	sus

Mine, yours, ours — other belonging words

These words always come after the noun.

	masculine singular	feminine singular	masculine plural	feminine plural
mine	mío	mía	míos	mías
yours (informal)	tuyo	tuya	tuyos	tuyas
his/hers/yours/theirs	suyo	suya	suyos	suyas

¿Esa casa es tuya? = Is that house yours?

If you're using belonging words on their own to mean 'mine' and you don't use the noun, you need to use the article as well as the 'mío' or 'mía'.

	masculine singular	feminine singular	masculine plural	feminine plural
mine (i.e. the one that's mine)	el mío	la mía	los míos	las mías
yours	el tuyo	la tuya	los tuyos	las tuyas
his/hers/yours/theirs	el suyo	la suya	los suyos	las suyas

No, la mía es más grande. = No, mine is bigger.

¿Esos guantes son suyos? = Are those gloves hers?

No, los suyos son verdes. = No, hers are green.

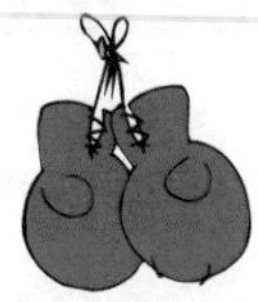

Use 'nuestro' for 'ours' and 'vuestro' for 'yours (plural)' and remember to choose the ending to match the object.

¿Ese hotel es vuestro? = Is that hotel yours?

No, el nuestro está cerca de la playa. = No, ours is near the beach.

To say 'whose', use 'cuyo'

The Spanish for 'whose' is 'cuyo/a/os/as'. The ending agrees with the thing that belongs to the person, not with the person it belongs to.

	masculine singular	feminine singular	masculine plural	feminine plural
whose	cuyo	cuya	cuyos	cuyas

Esa es la mujer cuyo marido es peruano. = That's the woman whose husband is Peruvian.

My, this stuff's certainly worth learning...

This page is full of things you really need to know — belonging words come up all the time in Spanish GCSE. Make sure you're clear on the difference between 'my', 'mine' and 'my one'.

ADVERBS

Making Sentences More Interesting

The pages before this are about describing objects (e.g. the bus is red). This page is about describing things you do (e.g. I speak Spanish well) and adding more info (e.g. I speak Spanish very well).

Make your sentences better by saying how you do things

1) In English, you don't say 'We talk slow', you have to add a 'ly' on the end to say 'We talk slowly'.
2) In Spanish, you have to add a 'mente' on the end, but first you have to make sure the describing word is in the feminine form (see p. 83).

The Spanish word for 'slow' is 'lento', but the feminine form is 'lenta'. Add 'mente' and you get 'lentamente' = slowly.

Habla lentamente. = He speaks slowly.

quickly:	rápidamente
normally:	normalmente

3) Unlike normal describing words (see p. 83) you don't ever have to change these words — even if what it's about is feminine or plural.

Hablamos lentamente. = We speak slowly.

Learn these odd ones out off by heart

Just like in English there are odd ones out — for example, you don't say I sing 'goodly'...

Spanish Odd Ones Out

ENGLISH	SPANISH
good → well	bueno/a → bien
bad → badly	malo/a → mal

Canto. I sing.

Canto bien. I sing well.

Canto mal. I sing badly.

Say when and where you do things

Here are some more handy little words you can stick into sentences to say when and where things happen:

here:	aquí	*now:*	ahora
there:	allí	*already:*	ya

Mi tía trabaja aquí. = My aunt works here.

Ya tengo un reloj. = I already have a watch.

Vamos a cenar ahora. = We're going to have dinner now.

Use these four words to give even more detail

Stick one of these four words in front of the describing word in a sentence to add extra detail and impress the examiners.

very:	muy	*almost:*	casi
quite:	bastante	*too:*	demasiado

Ella habla casi perfectamente el español. = She speaks Spanish almost perfectly.

Bob está muy feliz. = Bob is very happy.

Revise this lot really well, right here, right now...

Alrighty — this is a bit like English — you have a set ending (-mente) to learn and stick on, and it's not too tricky either. Make sure you really know the standard rule and all the exceptions.

Comparing Things

COMPARATIVES AND SUPERLATIVES

Saying something's good is easy enough, but what if you want to say it's better, or the best thing ever...

How to say 'more ...' and 'the most ...'

In Spanish you can't say 'stranger' or 'strangest', it's gotta be 'more strange' or 'the most strange':

Esta falda es cara. = This skirt is expensive.

Esta falda es más cara. = This skirt is more expensive.

Esta falda es la más cara. = This skirt is the most expensive.

fat:	gordo	*fatter:*	más gordo	*fattest:*	el más gordo
tall:	alto	*taller:*	más alto	*tallest:*	el más alto
big:	grande	*bigger:*	más grande	*biggest:*	el más grande

You can do this with almost any describing word. Don't forget to change the 'o' ending to 'a' for feminine and add 's' or 'es' for plural.

To say 'the most...' you have to use 'la más' or 'los/las más' if the word you're describing is feminine or plural.

Liz es la más alta. = Liz is the tallest.

Ed y Jo son los más altos. = Ed and Jo are the tallest.

BUT, just like in English, there are odd ones out:

good:	bueno	*better:*	mejor	*best:*	el mejor
bad:	malo	*worse:*	peor	*worst:*	el peor
old:	viejo	*older:*	mayor	*oldest:*	el mayor
young:	joven	*younger:*	menor	*youngest:*	el menor

El gorro azul es el mejor. = The blue cap is the best.

More and most with adverbs is pretty much the same...

When you're saying that someone does something more or most ...ly, you follow the same pattern as above, but instead of adjectives (describing words — see p. 83-85), you use adverbs (see p. 86).

Penélope trabaja alegremente. = Penélope works cheerfully.

Anita trabaja más alegremente. = Anita works more cheerfully.

Esteban es el que trabaja más alegremente. = Esteban works the most cheerfully / Esteban is the one who works the most cheerfully.

For a woman, change 'el que' to 'la que', and for groups change to 'los que' (or 'las que' if everyone in the group is female).

There are two odd ones out you need to know:

well: bien → *better:* mejor   *badly:* mal → *worse:* peor

Learn these three great ways of comparing things

Use 'más...que' ('more...than'), 'menos...que' ('less...than') and 'tan...como' ('as...as') to compare things.

Ed es más joven que Tom. = Ed is younger than Tom.

Ed es menos joven que Tom. = Ed is less young than Tom.

Ed es tan joven como Tom. = Ed is as young as Tom.

Wow, this is just super(lative)...

Make sure you learn how to say bigger or biggest, and how to say bigger than, as big as and less big than. And don't just learn the rule, learn all those exceptions to it as well.

CONJUNCTIONS

Joining Words — Longer Sentences

Everyone knows long sentences are clever — and examiners like clever people. So learn these joining words to help you make longer sentences, and get more marks for being smart.

Y = And

Me gusta jugar al fútbol. AND *Me gusta jugar al rugby.* = *Me gusta jugar al fútbol **y** al rugby.*

= I like playing football. = I like playing rugby. = I like playing football and rugby.

BUT: if 'y' comes in front of a word beginning with 'i' or 'hi' it changes to 'e'. *Hablo español e inglés.* = I speak Spanish and English.

O = Or

Juega al fútbol todos los días. OR *Juega al rugby todos los días.* = *Juega al fútbol **o** al rugby todos los días.*

= He plays football every day. = He plays rugby every day. = He plays football or rugby every day.

BUT: when 'o' comes in front of a word beginning with 'o' or 'ho' it changes to 'u'. *Cuesta siete u ocho libras.* = It costs seven or eight pounds.

Pero = But

Don't confuse 'pero' with 'perro' (dog).

Me gusta jugar al fútbol. BUT *No me gusta jugar al rugby.* = *Me gusta jugar al fútbol **pero** no me gusta jugar al rugby.*

= I like playing football. = I don't like playing rugby. = I like playing football but I don't like playing rugby.

When 'but' means 'on the contrary' it becomes 'sino': *Mi amigo no es americano **sino** australiano.* = My friend isn't American, but (on the contrary) he's Australian.

Porque = Because

This is a really important one you need to use to explain yourself. There's loads more about it on p. 8.

*Me gusta el tenis **porque** es divertido.* = I like tennis because it's fun.

Other joining words to understand

You don't have to use all of these, but you should understand them if you see or hear them.

well, then:	pues, entonces
if:	si
with:	con
as, like:	como
so, therefore:	por lo tanto, así (que), de manera (que)
while, during:	mientras
when:	cuando

*Puedes salir **si** quieres.* = You can go out if you want.

*Tengo hambre, **así que** voy a comer.* = I'm hungry, so I'm going to eat.

*Es **como** su hermano.* = He's like his brother.

*Va a la playa **cuando** hace sol.* = She goes to the beach when it's sunny.

I'd prefer a reduced sentence...

You use 'and', 'or', 'but' and 'because' all the time when you're speaking English — if you don't use them when you speak Spanish, it'll sound a bit weird. But don't confuse 'si' (if) and 'sí' (yes). It's good if you can recognise all the extra words in the last bit too, and it's even better if you can use them.

Sneaky Wee Words

PREPOSITIONS

You've got to learn these if you want tip-top marks. They're really useful words anyway.

TO — a, hasta

For 'the train to London' use 'the train for London' — see next page.

'To' is usually 'a':

*Va **a** Madrid.* = He's going to Madrid.

*Voy **a** casa.* = I'm going (to) home.

Or use 'hasta' when 'to' means 'as far as':

*Sólo va **hasta** York.* = He's only going to York.

ON — sobre, en

For 'on top of', it's 'sobre' or 'en':

Sobre la mesa. = On the table.

When it's not 'on top of', it's usually 'en':

*Lo vi **en** la tele.* = I saw it on TV.

For days of the week, it's left out:

Me voy el lunes. = I'm leaving on Monday.

IN — en, dentro de

'En' is just 'in', 'inside' is usually 'dentro de'.

*Está **en/dentro de** la caja.* = It's in(side) the box.

If it's in a town, it's 'en':

*Vivo **en** Málaga.* = I live in Malaga.

Don't forget to add 'en' when going into a place:

*Entra **en** la tienda.* = She enters (into) the shop.

FROM — de, desde or a partir de

Where we use 'from', they usually use 'de':

*Soy **de** Cardiff.* = I come from Cardiff.

'Desde' is used where there is a starting and finishing point:

Desde Londres hasta Madrid. = From London to Madrid.

For dates, it's 'a partir de':

A partir del 4 de junio. = From the 4th of June.

OF — de

Where we use 'of', they usually use 'de':

*Una botella **de** leche.* = A bottle of milk.

'Made of' is 'de':

*Es un cinturón **de** cuero.* = It's a leather belt.

WATCH OUT: sometimes it's hard to spot the de in a sentence, because de + el = del.

*Salgo **del** supermercado.* = I go out of the supermarket.

AT — en, a

Most English phrases with 'at' in them use 'en' in the Spanish — a few use 'a'.

A las seis. = At six o'clock.

*Ella está **en** la escuela.* = She is at school.

En casa. = At home.

Don't forget — a + el = al. Sometimes it can be tricky to spot.

Learn these words for saying where something is

You need these little words a lot, for saying where things are in your town or your house.

*El banco está **enfrente del** hotel.* = The bank is opposite the hotel.

next to:	al lado de	*on / upon:*	en, sobre	*at the back of:*	al fondo de
behind:	detrás de	*above:*	encima de	*here:*	aquí
in front of:	delante de	*against:*	contra	*there:*	allí, ahí, allá
between:	entre	*in / into:*	en	*inside:*	dentro de
under / below:	bajo/debajo de	*at the end of:*	al final de	*outside:*	fuera de

Don't forget to use está / están for describing where things are.

Of, at, in, from, shake it all about...

Prepositions have loads of different meanings in English — it's important to remember they do in Spanish too, just not the same ones. You have to learn the words from a Spanish perspective.

'POR' & 'PARA'

'Por' and 'Para'

'Por' and 'para' are two nightmare words for English speakers because they both mean 'for' — but in different ways. This bit's going to be tricky I'm afraid, but it's really important — it's worth learning.

Use Para for...

1) Saying who something is for: *Este dinero es para ti.* = This money is for you.
2) Talking about destination: *El tren para Buenos Aires.* = The train to Buenos Aires.
3) When you want to say 'to'/'in order to': *Se fue de vacaciones para descansar.* = He went on holiday in order to rest.
4) When you want to say 'by' in time phrases: *para mañana* = by / for tomorrow *para entonces* = by / for then
5) 'For' in sentences like 'for X days' when you're talking about the future: *Quiero el coche para tres días.* = I want the car for three days.
6) 'In (my / your...) view': *Para mí, ella es la chica más atractiva de todas.* = In my view, she's the most attractive girl of all.
7) 'About to': *Está para llover.* = It's about to rain.

Confusingly, in Latin America they use 'por' for 'about to'.

Use Por for...

1) 'For' in time sentences, like 'for X months / years' in the past or future: *Vivió en Málaga por un año.* = He lived in Malaga for a year.
2) 'In' to talk about parts of the day: *por la mañana* = in the morning
3) When you say 'through': *El tren va por el túnel.* = The train goes through the tunnel.
4) 'Per' in number phrases: *dos veces por día* = twice a day *veinte por ciento* = twenty percent
5) Exchange: *Pagó diez euros por el libro.* = He paid 10 euros for the book.
6) On behalf of: *Lo hizo por ti.* = He did it for you.
7) When you say 'gracias': *Gracias por todos los peces.* = Thanks for all the fish.

Por and para — wish I knew what they're for...

This is possibly the trickiest thing in the whole of GCSE Spanish — in fact it might be the hardest thing to get your head around in Spanish full stop. All you can do is learn and apply the rules — learning the examples will really help you to understand the difference between 'por' and 'para'.

I, You, Him, Them...

PRONOUNS

Pronouns are really handy words that save you from having to keep repeating nouns all the time.

Yo, tú, él, ella... — I, you, he, she...

Pronouns are words that replace nouns — like 'you' or 'them'.

Kelly has a new job at the wig factory.
She likes making wigs.

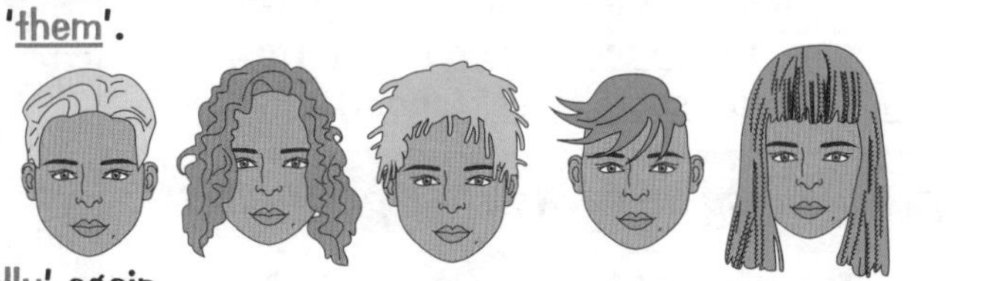

'She' is a pronoun. It means you don't have to say 'Kelly' again.

'I', 'you', 'he', etc. are not usually needed in Spanish — unless you want to emphasise or make it clear exactly who you're talking about. You need to know them though — or you'll end up getting seriously confused.

THE SUBJECT PRONOUNS

I:	yo	we:	nosotros/as
you (informal singular):	tú	you (informal plural):	vosotros/as
he / it:	él	they (masculine or mixed masculine and feminine):	ellos
she / it:	ella	they (all feminine):	ellas
you (formal singular):	usted	you (formal plural):	ustedes
one:	se		

THE FOUR 'YOU's

Remember — there are 4 ways of talking to 'you'. 'Tú' is for one person who's your friend, a member of your family or about your age. For a group of people you know, use 'vosotros/as'. You use 'usted' to be polite to one person (for older people who aren't your family or friends), or 'ustedes' if there's more than one of them.

Me, te, lo... — me, you, him...

These are for the person / thing in a sentence that's having the action done to it (the direct object).

Dave lava el perro. → *Dave lo lava.*

= Dave washes the dog. = Dave washes it.

THE DIRECT OBJECT PRONOUNS

me:	me	us:	nos
you (informal singular):	te	you (informal plural):	os
him / it / you (formal singular masculine):	lo	them / you (formal plural masculine):	los
her / it / you (formal singular feminine):	la	them / you (formal plural feminine):	las

There are special words for to me, to her, to them

For things that need 'to' or 'for' — like writing to someone — use the indirect object pronouns.

El perro da el cepillo a Dave. = The dog gives the brush to Dave.

El perro le da el cepillo. = The dog gives the brush to him.

THE INDIRECT OBJECT PRONOUNS

to me:	me
to you (informal singular):	te
to him / her / it / you (formal singular):	le
to us:	nos
to you (informal plural or formal):	os
to them / you (formal plural):	les

These pronouns usually come before the verb, but when you tell someone to do something they are tacked on to the end of the verb.

¡Llámame! = Call me!

You'll definitely need these pronouns for saying you like something. You have to say 'it is pleasing to me' etc. It doesn't matter if the person is singular or plural — you need 'gusta' if the thing you like is singular, or 'gustan' if it's plural.

No nos gusta el pulpo. = We don't like octopus.

¿Te gustan los árboles? = Do you like trees?

Four yous — you should see a therapist about that...

This stuff is really worth learning. If you skip it, you'll end up with sentences like: "Harry went to the pet shop and Harry saw a dog and Harry liked the dog so Harry bought the dog" — not ideal.

PREPOSITIONAL & RELATIVE PRONOUNS, PRONOUN ORDER

More on Pronouns

Sometimes you'll need the pronouns on the first bit of this page — they can be a bit confusing, so learn them.

Special words for me, you, him, her...

There are some pronouns that change when they come after a preposition like 'a' (to), 'para' (for), or 'sobre' / 'de' (about):

*El regalo no es para **ti**, es para **ella**.*

= The present isn't for you, it's for her.

PREPOSITIONAL PRONOUNS

me:	mí	*us:*	nosotros/as
you (informal singular):	ti	*you (informal plural):*	vosotros/as
him/it:	él	*them (masc. or mixed):*	ellos
her/it:	ella	*them (all feminine):*	ellas
you (formal singular):	usted	*you (formal plural):*	ustedes

'With me' and 'with you' (familiar singular) have their own special words: *with me:* conmigo *with you:* contigo

The personal 'a'

You need to put an extra 'a' in before the word for any human being after every single verb except 'tener'. It sounds confusing but it isn't:

*Estoy buscando **a** Juan.* = I'm looking for Juan. BUT *Estoy buscando un taxi.* = I'm looking for a taxi.

Que — that, which, who

'Que' is a special kind of pronoun (a relative pronoun). It can mean 'which', 'who', or 'that'.

*Fui a Menorca, **que** es una isla preciosa.* = I went to Menorca, which is a lovely island.

For ideas rather than objects, use 'lo que':

*Van a venir, **lo que** es maravilloso.* = They're going to come, which is wonderful.

After a preposition, use 'quien' (who), 'el que' or 'el cual' (that) instead of 'que'.

Use la que or la cual for feminine and los/las que or los/las cuales for plural.

*el hombre **a quien** vimos* = the man whom we saw

*la película de **la que** estoy hablando.* = the film that I'm talking about.

that (more formal): la cual

Getting the Order Right

1) These pronouns usually go before the verb — though they can go before OR on the end of an infinitive or a present participle:

Lo estamos mirando. / Estamos mirándolo. = We're watching it.

...and they must go after a command to do something: *Deme su pasaporte.* = Give me your passport.

2) Whenever there are two object pronouns in the same sentence, the indirect ones always go first:

Te la enviaré. = I'll send it to you. *Me los da.* = He gives them to me.

3) But, if the indirect pronoun is 'le' or 'les', it changes to 'se' when it comes in front of lo, la, los or las.

Se lo regalé. = I gave it to him / her / them / you.

It could be any one of these — you need to look at the sentences around to work out who it's on about.

A's back — and this time it's personal...

There's loads of lovely stuff to learn on this page. Have fun learning it all.

This & That, Something & Someone

Demonstratives & Indefinite Pronouns

This page is about pointing things out, and generally making it clear which thing you're on about.

How to say this, that or that over there

Use 'este', etc. for saying things like 'this man', 'these apples' (when you're using 'this' as a describing word).

	Masculine singular	Feminine singular		Masculine plural	Feminine plural
THIS	este	esta	THESE	estos	estas
THAT	ese	esa	THOSE	esos	esas
THAT (further away)	aquel	aquella	THOSE (further away)	aquellos	aquellas

este pájaro = this bird

aquella casa = that house

estas manzanas = these apples

esos bolis = those pens

Use the neuter when you're not talking about a particular thing:

	Neuter
THIS	esto
THAT	eso / aquello

¿Qué es esto? = What's this?

¡Eso es! = That's it!

It's different when you use 'this' or 'these' as a noun

When you say things like 'this is mine', you're using 'this' as a noun. That means you need to stick an accent on the 'this' word: e.g. éstos, ése etc, except if it's used at the beginning of the sentence.

Tengo dos perros: éste es simpático, pero ése es malo.

= I've got two dogs: this one here is nice, but that one is nasty.

Aquella casa es más grande que ésta. = That house over there is bigger than this one.

Algo — Something Alguien — Someone

There's nothing particularly special about these, you just need to be able to understand and use them:

Hay algo en mi bolsa.

= There's something in my bag.

¿Quiere algo?

= Do you want something?

Buscan a alguien con el pelo largo.

See p. 92 for more on the personal 'a'.

= They're looking for someone with long hair.

Alguien ha llevado el dinero. = Someone has taken the money.

So, what are you studying? Oh, this and that...

None of this stuff is too tricky — as long as you're absolutely one hundred percent sure you've got it clear. Remember — 'este', 'esa' and the others always go with another word, like 'este hombre'. If they're on their own, they must have accents ('éste', 'ésa' etc.)— so don't forget 'em.

VERBS, TENSES AND THE INFINITIVE

The Lowdown on Verbs

Oh boy — you just can't get away from this stuff, I'm afraid.
But think about this — if you learn it now, it'll make the whole of Spanish GCSE easier...

Verbs are action words — they tell you what's going on

Ethel ***plays*** *football every Saturday.*

Alex ***wished*** *his grandma* ***preferred*** *knitting.*

These are verbs.

And so is this.

There's a load of stuff you need to know about verbs, but it all boils down to these two things...

1) The verb is different for different times

You say things differently if they happened last week, or aren't going to happen till tomorrow.

HAS ALREADY HAPPENED
I went to Tibet last year.
I have been to Tibet.
I had been to Tibet.
I used to go to Tibet.

PAST

HAPPENING NOW
I go to Tibet.
I am going to Tibet.

PRESENT

HASN'T HAPPENED YET
I go to Tibet on Monday.
I will go to Tibet.
I will be going to Tibet.
I am going to Tibet on Monday.
I am going to go to Tibet.

FUTURE

These are all different tenses, in case you're interested.

2) The verb is different for different people

You'd say 'he plays', but never 'I plays' — it'd be daft. The verb changes to fit the person.

HAPPENING TO ME
I am miserable.

HAPPENING TO YOU
You are miserable.

HAPPENING TO HER
She is miserable.

OK, you get the picture — verbs are dead important. You use them all the time, after all.

The infinitive means 'to...'

When you look up a verb in the dictionary, this is what you get:

(to) give: dar
(to) go: ir

In Spanish, infinitives always end in 'r'.

Most of the time, you won't want the verb in its raw state — you'll have to change it so it's right for the person and time you're talking about.

BUT: if you want to use two verbs together, the second one usually needs to be infinitive.

Quiero ***comer***. = I want to eat.

Preferimos ***bailar***. = We prefer to dance.

So I guess you could call action films 'verb films'...

I'm not kidding — this is mega-important stuff. Over the next few pages I'll give you loads of stuff on verbs because there's loads you need to know. Some of it's easy, some of it's tricky — but if you don't understand the things on this page before you start, you'll have no chance.

Verbs in the Present Tense

PRESENT TENSE

Sadly, this is nothing to do with Christmas gifts — it's the easiest of the verb forms in Spanish. That doesn't mean you can skip it though — you've still got to get it right.

The present tense is what's happening now

You'll use it more than anything else, so it's really important. It's all about sticking 'endings' onto something (the 'stem').

Formula for Present Tense Stems

stem = infinitive – last two letters

Example of Present Tense Stems

Infinitive	hablar	comer	vivir
Stem	habl	com	viv

For the present tense, the 'stems' that you stick the endings onto are dead easy:

Endings for -ar verbs

To form the present tense of regular '-ar' verbs, add the following endings to the verb's stem — e.g.:

HABLAR = TO SPEAK

I speak:	habl**o**	*we speak:*	habl**amos**
you (informal singular) speak:	habl**as**	*you (informal plural) speak:*	habl**áis**
he / she / it speaks:	habl**a**	*they speak:*	habl**an**
you (formal singular) speak:	habl**a**	*you (formal plural) speak:*	habl**an**

See p. 91 for when to use which form of 'you'.

So if you want to say something like 'He talks a lot', it's dead easy:

1) Start by knocking off the 'ar': habl~~ar~~
2) Then add on the new ending: habl ← a
3) And — ta da... *Habla mucho.* = He talks a lot.

Endings for -er verbs

To form the present tense of regular '-er' verbs, add the following endings to the verb's stem — e.g.:

The first bit ('com') doesn't change.

COMER = TO EAT

I eat:	com**o**	*we eat:*	com**emos**
you (informal singular) eat:	com**es**	*you (informal plural) eat:*	com**éis**
he / she / it eats:	com**e**	*they eat:*	com**en**
you (formal singular) eat:	com**e**	*you (formal plural) eat:*	com**en**

Endings for -ir verbs

To form the present tense of regular '-ir' verbs, add the following endings to the verb's stem — e.g.:

He, she, it and you (usted) always have the same ending.

VIVIR = TO LIVE

I live:	viv**o**	*we live:*	viv**imos**
you (informal singular) live:	viv**es**	*you (informal plural) live:*	viv**ís**
he / she / it lives:	viv**e**	*they live:*	viv**en**
you (formal singular) live:	viv**e**	*you (formal plural) live:*	viv**en**

They and you (formal plural) always have the same ending.

Present tense — the gift that keeps on giving...

All you have to do is learn the endings for '-ar', '-er' & '-ir' verbs. They aren't too bad, really, because a lot of the '-er' and '-ir' endings are the same. Learn them all and practise them.

PRESENT TENSE

Verbs in the Present Tense

OK, on the last page you got the nice regular verbs. Now you get the horrible irregular ones. Enjoy.

Some Spanish Verbs are almost Irregular

1) Some verbs change their spelling in the present tense. These are called stem or radical changing verbs.
2) They change the 'e' in their stem to an 'ie' or the 'o' or 'u' to a 'ue'.
3) Stem changing verbs don't change in the 'nosotros' (we) and 'vosotros' (you — informal plural) forms.
4) The person endings are regular, even though the stem is irregular.

Example of 'e' to 'ie' verbs:

QUERER = TO WANT

I want	= quiero
you want	= quieres
he / she / it wants / you (formal singular) want	= quiere
we want	= queremos
you (informal plural) want	= queréis
they / you (formal plural) want	= quieren

INFINITIVE	'I' PERSON
cerrar *(to close)*	*cierro*
comenzar *(to begin)*	*comienzo*
empezar *(to begin)*	*empiezo*
pensar *(to think)*	*pienso*
preferir *(to prefer)*	*prefiero*
sentarse *(to sit down)*	*me siento*
sentir *(to feel)*	*siento*
tener *(to have)*	*tengo (tú tienes)*
venir *(to come)*	*vengo (tú vienes)*

These two are irregular in the 'I' part too.

Example of 'o' to 'ue' verbs:

PODER = TO BE ABLE TO

I can	= puedo
you can	= puedes
he / she / it / you (formal singular) can	= puede
we can	= podemos
you (informal plural) can	= podéis
they / you (formal plural) can	= pueden

INFINITIVE	'I' PERSON
acostarse *(to go to bed)*	*me acuesto*
almorzar *(to have lunch)*	*almuerzo*
costar *(to cost)*	*cuesta (it costs)*
doler *(to hurt)*	*duele (it hurts)*
dormir *(to sleep)*	*duermo*
jugar *(to play)*	*juego*
llover *(to rain)*	*llueve (it rains)*
morir *(to die)*	*muero*
volver *(to return)*	*vuelvo*

Some of the most Useful Verbs are totally Irregular

Here are three irregular verbs. They happen to be three of the most important Spanish verbs ever — typical.

SER = TO BE

I am	= **soy**
you are	= **eres**
he / she / it is / you (formal singular) are	= **es**
we are	= **somos**
you (informal plural) are	= **sois**
they / you (formal plural) are	= **son**

ESTAR = TO BE

I am	= **estoy**
you are	= **estás**
he / she / it is / you (formal singular) are	= **está**
we are	= **estamos**
you (informal plural) are	= **estáis**
they / you (formal plural) are	= **están**

There are two different verbs for 'to be' in Spanish. Weird or what? You can find out all about them on the next page.

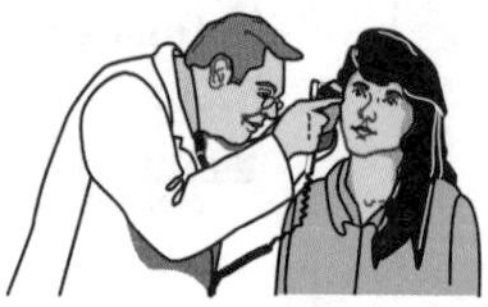

IR = TO GO

I go	= **voy**
you go	= **vas**
he / she / it goes / you (formal singular) go	= **va**
we go	= **vamos**
you (informal plural) go	= **vais**
they / you (formal plural) go	= **van**

A secret blend of verbs makes this book taste great...

Irregular verbs might be a bit more difficult than regular ones, but they're still learnable.

'Ser' and 'Estar'

Here's where things get even more complicated. One verb for 'to be' just isn't enough for Spanish speakers, so they've got two — the greedy things.

Ser and Estar both mean To Be

'Ser' and 'estar' both mean 'to be' in Spanish, but they're used differently — you can't just use whichever one you prefer.
It can be difficult to know which one to use when, but there are a few rules to help.

Use Ser for Permanent things

Use ser to talk about things that don't change.

1) Nationalities:

Somos peruanos. = We are Peruvian.

Clare es de Escocia. = Clare is from Scotland.

2) Saying who someone is (names, family relationships, etc.):

Ese chico es mi primo. = That boy is my cousin.

Soy Julieta. = I'm Julieta.

3) Jobs:

La señora Mitchell es profesora de español. = Mrs Mitchell is a Spanish teacher.

4) Physical characteristics:

Mis ojos son verdes. = My eyes are green.

Sois altos. = You (plural) are tall.

5) Personality:

Eres muy inteligente. = You are very intelligent.

Mis hermanas son alegres. = My sisters are cheerful. (i.e. they are cheerful people)

Use Estar for Temporary things and Locations

Use estar to talk about things that are true at the moment, but might change in the future:

Está enfermo. = He is ill.

Estás muy guapa. = You look very beautiful.

'Eres muy guapa' would mean 'you are (always) very beautiful'.

Mi profesor está alegre hoy. = My teacher is cheerful today (but he might not be tomorrow).

Estar is also used to say where someone or something is:

Madrid está en España. = Madrid is in Spain.

Estamos en casa. = We are at home.

"To be or to be" — that's the real question...

Yep, it's a bit of a pain having two ways of saying 'to be', but the difference is actually quite straightforward — use 'ser' if it's permanent and 'estar' if it's temporary or a place, and you won't go too far wrong. Just keep going over the examples on this page until it all becomes clear.

FUTURE AND IMMEDIATE FUTURE

Talking About the Future

You'll need to talk about things that are going to happen at some point in the future.
There are two ways you can do it — and the first one's a piece of cake...

You can use 'I'm going to' to talk about the future

Saying you're going to do something is pretty much the same in Spanish as in English. You just need the bit of 'ir' (to go) that goes with the person you're talking about, then 'a' and a verb in the infinitive. It's called the immediate future tense, but you don't have to be talking about something that's about to happen.

Immediate future tense = 'ir' in the present tense + a + infinitive

IR = TO GO

I am going	voy
you (inf. sing.) are going	vas
he / she / it is going	va
you (form. sing.) are going	va
we are going	vamos
you (inf. plu.) are going	vais
they / you (form. plu.) are going	van

Ella va a leer un libro. = She is going to read a book.

El sábado, vamos a ir a Francia. = On Saturday, we are going to go to France.

Put in phrases to say when you're going to do it (see p. 2–3).

You need to know the Proper Future Tense too

You can use the proper future tense to say 'I will do something' rather than 'I'm going to do it'.
This is another one of those tenses where it's all about sticking endings onto something (the 'stem').
Luckily, the future tense endings are the same for all verbs, whether they're -ar, -er or -ir verbs:

FUTURE TENSE ENDINGS

I:	-é	*we:*	-emos
you (informal):	-ás	*you (inf. plu.):*	-éis
he / she / it / you (form. sing.):	-á	*they / you (form. plu.):*	-án

The 'stems' that you stick the endings onto are pretty easy too:

For most verbs, you just stick the ending onto the infinitive (see p. 94).

Jugaré al tenis. = I will play tennis.

Dormirás. = You will sleep.

Cogerá el autobús. = He will take the bus.

Venderemos el perro. = We will sell the dog.

There are a few verbs that don't follow the pattern, so you have to learn them off by heart. These are the most important ones:

VERB	'I' PERSON	VERB	'I' PERSON	VERB	'I' PERSON
decir	diré	*poner*	pondré	*salir*	saldré
haber	habré	*querer*	querré	*poder*	podré
hacer	haré	*saber*	sabré		
tener	tendré	*venir*	vendré		

Look into my crystal ball...

OK, so the top one's easier, because you only have to learn the words for times in the future and bung them in a sentence. The proper future tense is harder — but it'll win you more marks if you use it. Make sure you at least understand it, in case it crops up in your reading or listening papers.

Conditional Tense

CONDITIONAL

Now it's time to talk about what could or would happen in the future.

The Conditional Tense — What would you do?

The conditional tense (for saying 'would') uses the same stems as the future tense (see p. 98) and adds these endings:

CONDITIONAL TENSE ENDINGS

I:	-ía	we:	-íamos
you (informal):	-ías	you (inf. plu.):	-íais
he / she / it / you (form. sing.):	-ía	they / you (form. plu.):	-ían

These are the same as the imperfect tense endings for -er and -ir verbs (see p. 103).

Compraría un helado. = I would buy an ice-cream.

¿Podría usted ayudarme? = Could you help me?

You can combine the conditional with other tenses to make more complicated sentences:

Bailaría, pero me duelen los pies. = I would dance, but my feet hurt.

Les gustaría ir a la playa, pero no pueden ir porque está lloviendo.

= They would like to go to the beach, but they can't go because it's raining.

If you want to seriously wow the examiners, use the conditional tense of 'haber' (to have...) with the past participle (see p. 100) to mean 'would have...'.

Habría comprado un libro. = I would have bought a book.

A couple of Alternatives to the Conditional

Two really common verbs sometimes get replaced in the conditional by a different form.

1) The conditional form of 'querer' (to want) is often replaced by 'quisiera'.

querría → quisiera

You can use 'quisiera' in polite requests to mean 'I would like'.

Quisiera reservar una mesa para tres personas.

= I would like to reserve a table for three.

'Quisiera' and 'hubiera' are in the imperfect subjunctive. See p. 106 for more.

2) The conditional of 'haber' (to have...) can be replaced by 'hubiera'.

You probably won't come across this, but it's good to be prepared just in case.

habría → hubiera

Hubiera venido antes. = I would have come earlier.

Shampoo and conditional — for softer, silkier verbs...

Make sure you don't get confused between the conditional and the future or the imperfect.

PERFECT TENSE

Talking About the Past

Uh oh, it's the first of several past tenses now. The main thing is you need to make sure you can tell it apart from the future (p. 98) and the present (p. 95) tenses. You don't want to be stuck not knowing whether something has happened, is happening or is going to happen.

¿Qué has hecho? — What have you done?

You have to be able to make and understand sentences like this:

There are two important bits.

He jugado al tenis. = I have played tennis.

This is the Perfect Tense.

1) You always need a bit to mean 'I have' — see the next page.

2) This bit means 'played'. It's a special version of 'jugar' (to play). In English, most of these words end in '-ed'. See below.

Jugado = played: special past tense words

Learn the patterns for making the special past tense words like 'jugado' (played).

-AR VERBS

Remove '-ar', then add '-ado':

jugar / jugado	to play / played
esperar / esperado	to wait / waited

-ER/-IR VERBS

Remove '-er' or '-ir' then add '-ido':

vender / vendido	to sell / sold
beber / bebido	to drink / drunk
salir / salido	to leave / left
elegir / elegido	to choose / chosen

The words for 'played', 'drunk', 'chosen', etc. are called past participles.

Some verbs don't follow the patterns. It's dead annoying, because a lot of the most useful verbs are irregular — you just have to learn them off by heart:

Verb	Past tense version (past participle)	English
abrir:	abierto	*opened*
cubrir:	cubierto	*covered*
decir:	dicho	*said*
descubrir:	descubierto	*knew / discovered*
escribir:	escrito	*written*
hacer:	hecho	*done / made*
poner:	puesto	*put*
romper:	roto	*broken*
ver:	visto	*seen*
volver:	vuelto	*returned*

That's all perfectly clear...

OK, this page isn't easy — no sireee. But it's dead important — in the exams, you'll need to talk or write about something that's happened in the past if you want a top grade. Scribble down the table of past participles and learn it really well — they'll come in handy for other verb forms too.

Talking About the Past

PERFECT & PLUPERFECT

Now that you can form past participles, you can use them to say what you have done or had done.

He hecho — I have done

You use the perfect tense to say you have done something. You need the present tense of 'haber' and the past participle.

Perfect tense = present tense of 'haber' + past participle

The past participle (like 'jugado' or 'hecho') always stays the same — you don't need to make it feminine or plural. Only the 'haber' part changes depending on who's doing the action.

HABER = TO HAVE...	
I have...	he
you (inf. sing.) have...	has
he / she / it has...	ha
you (form. sing.) have...	ha
we have...	hemos
you (inf. plu.) have...	habéis
they / you (form. plu.) have...	han

He ido al cine. = I have been to the cinema.

Han jugado al tenis. = They have played tennis.

¿Has roto el vaso? = Have you broken the glass?

If you want to be really fancy, you can use the perfect tense in sentences with other tenses.

Me gustaría ir a Méjico porque nunca he estado allí.

= I'd like to go to Mexico because I've never been there.

Había hecho — I had done

1) It's similar to the perfect tense, but this is for saying what you had done, not what you have done.
2) It's still made of a bit of haber and a past participle, but the bit of haber is in the imperfect tense (see p. 103 to learn all about the imperfect tense).

Pluperfect tense = imperfect tense of 'haber' + past participle

IMPERFECT OF HABER	
I had...	había
you (inf. sing.) had...	habías
he / she / it had...	había
you (form. sing.) had...	había
we had...	habíamos
you (inf. plu.) had...	habíais
they / you (form. plu.) had...	habían

Habían comprado una casa en España.

= They had bought a house in Spain.

Sue había llegado. = Sue had arrived.

You can use the pluperfect with other tenses too:

No fui al cine con mis amigos porque ya había visto la película.

= I didn't go to the cinema with my friends because I had seen the film already.

The perfect tense — you can't get better than that...

The perfect and pluperfect are really handy for talking about the past, and they're pretty straightforward once you get the hang of them. Make sure you learn the present and imperfect forms of 'haber' really well, and soon there'll be no stopping you. Perfect, you could say.

PRETERITE

Another Past Tense: 'Did'

The preterite tense (I went, etc.) is the most useful tense for talking about what happened in the past, but, guess what, it's the one with the most irregular bits. Make sure you learn this page carefully — you'll need it.

¿Qué hiciste después? — What did you do next?

This is like saying 'I did', rather than 'I have done' — just take the stem of the infinitive, and add these endings:

PRETERITE ENDINGS FOR '-AR' VERBS

I	-é	we	-amos
you (inf. singular)	-aste	you (inf. plural)	-asteis
he / she / it / you (form. singular)	-ó	they / you (form. plural)	-aron

PRETERITE ENDINGS FOR '-ER'/'-IR' VERBS

I	-í	we	-imos
you (inf. singular)	-iste	you (inf. plural)	-isteis
he / she / it / you (form. singular)	-ió	they / you (form. plural)	-ieron

Pasó toda la vida en Badajoz. = He spent all his life in Badajoz.

Nací en Portsmouth. = I was born in Portsmouth.

Bailamos hasta medianoche. = We danced until midnight.

The accents are really important. They can change the meaning of words:

Hablo con Susana. = I speak to Susana.

Habló con Susana. = He spoke to Susana.

There are four vital irregular verbs in the preterite

Typical — the words you'll need most often are the irregular ones. Make sure you get them learnt:

Ser — to be / Ir — to go (they have the same preterite)

I was	fui	we were	fuimos
you (inf.) were	fuiste	you (inf.) were	fuisteis
he / she / it was / you (form.) were	fue	they / you (form.) were	fueron

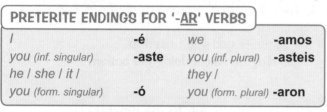

These Spanish words can also mean 'I went', 'you went', 'he went' etc. — you can tell whether it's 'ir' or 'ser' by the context.

Estar — to be

I was	estuve	we were	estuvimos
you (inf.) were	estuviste	you (inf.) were	estuvisteis
he / she / it was / you (form.) were	estuvo	they / you (form.) were	estuvieron

Hacer — to do or make

I did / made	hice	we did / made	hicimos
you (inf.) did / made	hiciste	you (inf.) did / made	hicisteis
he / she / it / you (form.) did / made	hizo	they / you (form.) did / made	hicieron

Here are some other common irregular ones that change their stem in the preterite:

Infinitives	yo	él/ella/usted
dar	di	dio
decir	dije	dijo
poder	pude	pudo
poner	puse	puso
querer	quise	quiso
tener	tuve	tuvo
traer	traje	trajo
venir	vine	vino

No me dieron nada. = They didn't give me anything.

Dijiste que te gustó. = You said that you liked it.

¿Adónde pusiste el queso? = Where did you put the cheese?

Hang on a second — I thought 'vino' was wine...

Yes, the word for 'he / she / it came' is exactly the same as the one for 'wine' in Spanish. It's a bit weird if you ask me, but at least it might help you remember the irregular preterite of 'venir'.

'Was Doing' or 'Used to Do'

Imperfect Tense

...And another tense for talking about the past — you lucky thing!

What you were doing or used to do

This is another dead useful one. There are 3 easy steps to making this tense:

1) Get the infinitive of the verb you want to use (see p. 94).
2) Knock the '-ar', '-er' or '-ir' off the end.
3) Add on the correct ending from the first or second list:

Imperfect Tense Endings for '-ar' verbs

I	-aba	*we*	-ábamos
you (inf. sing.)	-abas	*you (inf. plu.)*	-abais
he / she / it /		*they /*	
you (form. sing.)	-aba	*you (form. plu.)*	-aban

Imperfect Tense Endings for '-er' / '-ir' verbs

I	-ía	*we:*	-íamos
you (inf. sing.)	-ías	*you (inf. plu.)*	-íais
he / she / it /		*they /*	
you (form. sing.)	-ía	*you (form. plu.)*	-ían

Hablábamos por teléfono.

= We were talking / used to talk on the phone.

Hacía mucho deporte.

= I used to do a lot of sport.

Only 3 verbs don't follow the pattern — ser, ir, and ver. Ver is almost regular — just add normal '-er' endings onto 've-', e.g. 'veía'.

Mi padre era médico.

= My father was / used to be a doctor.

Ir = to go

I	iba
you	ibas
he / she / it	iba
you (form. sing.)	iba
we	íbamos
you (inf. plu.)	ibais
they / you (form. plu.)	iban

Ser = to be

I	era
you (inf. sing.)	eras
he / she / it	era
you (form. sing.)	era
we	éramos
you (inf. plu.)	erais
they / you (form. plu.)	eran

Había... — There was / There were...

In the present tense of haber, 'hay' means 'there is' or 'there are'. 'Había' is the imperfect version of 'hay', so it can mean 'there was' or 'there were' — it doesn't change.

Había un mono en el árbol.

= There was a monkey in the tree.

Había unas flores en el jardín.

= There were some flowers in the garden.

When to use the imperfect

1) What you used to do repeatedly in the past:

Iba al cine cada jueves. = I used to go to the cinema every Thursday.

2) Descriptions about something in the past: *Hacía mucho calor.* = It was very hot.

3) Saying what was going on when something else happened (use the preterite tense for the key event, and the imperfect tense for the background situation):

Saqué una foto mientras llovía.

= I took a photo while it was raining.

The imperfect — it's in-tense...

Don't be put off by the name — the imperfect's actually really good. So make sure you learn it.

REFLEXIVE VERBS

Myself, Yourself, etc.

Sometimes you'll have to talk about things you do to yourself — like 'washing yourself' or 'getting yourself up' in the morning. It sounds weird in English, but in Spanish they do it all the time.

Talking about yourself — me, te, se...

'Se' means 'oneself'. Here are all the different ways to say 'self':

myself:	me	*yourself (form. sing):*	se
yourself (inf.):	te	*ourselves:*	nos
himself:	se	*yourselves (inf. plu.):*	os
herself:	se	*themselves, each other:*	se
oneself:	se	*yourselves (form. plu.):*	se

You can tell which verbs need 'self' by checking in the dictionary. If you look up 'to get washed', it'll say 'lavarse'.

Reflexive verbs are really useful for talking about daily routine stuff... getting up, getting washed, etc. All you've got to do is learn the pattern — e.g. 'lavarse' = to get washed (literally 'to wash oneself'):

I get washed:	**me** lavo	*we get washed:*	**nos** lavamos
you get washed (informal singular):	**te** lavas	*you get washed (informal plural):*	**os** laváis
he / she / it gets washed:	**se** lava	*they get washed:*	**se** lavan
you get washed (formal singular):	**se** lava	*you get washed (formal plural):*	**se** lavan

There are lots of these verbs, but here are the ones you should know:

IMPORTANT REFLEXIVE VERBS

to go to bed:	acostarse	*to wake up:*	despertarse
to get up:	levantarse	*to go away:*	irse
to feel:	sentirse	*to get dressed:*	vestirse
to be called:	llamarse		

¿Te sientes mal? = Do you feel ill?

No me despierto temprano. = I don't wake up early.

Perfect tense reflexive verbs are pretty easy

When you want to use reflexive verbs in the perfect tense, you just put the 'me', 'se' or whatever in front of all the bits of the verb as usual:

Me he puesto el sombrero. = I've put my hat on.

Stick the 'me' at the start.

Then put the whole of the perfect tense verb (see p. 101).

¿Se habla español?

You can turn any Spanish verb into an impersonal verb (e.g. 'one does' rather than 'I do' or 'he does') by using 'se' and the he/she/it part of the verb:

¿Se puede comer afuera? = Can one eat outside?

If there's an object in the sentence, use the singular for a single object, and the plural for plural objects:

Las puertas se abren a las nueve. = The doors are opened at nine.

El arroz se cocina durante quince minutos. = The rice is cooked for 15 minutes.

The passive is another way of saying that something happens without saying who does it. It's formed using ser and the past participle (see p. 100). You don't need to use the passive, but you do need to recognise it.

La catedral fue construida en 1347. = The cathedral was built in 1347.

Talk about myself — don't mind if I do...

There's loads to learn on this page, but it's all incredibly useful, so make sure you learn everything.

How to say 'Not' & 'Nobody'

Negatives

You need to know how to say 'no' and 'not' and things in Spanish. You'd be in big trouble if a Mexican knife thrower asked you to be his assistant and you could only say yes...

Use 'no' to say not

In English you change a sentence to mean the opposite by adding 'not', e.g. 'I am Bob' ➡ 'I am not Bob'. In Spanish, you have to put 'no' in front of the action word (verb).

Soy Miguel. = I am Miguel. ➡ *No soy Miguel.* = I am not Miguel.

'Soy' is the verb. The 'no' goes in front — easy.

You do the same with all the tenses:

No voy a leer el periódico. = I'm not going to read the newspaper.

No fuimos al parque. = We did not go to the park.

No harán sus deberes. = They will not do their homework.

Ella no ha llegado. = She has not arrived.

No, I don't...

'No' in Spanish means both 'no' and 'not', so if you're answering a question, you may need to say 'no' twice:

No, no quiero pulpo, gracias. = No, I don't want any octopus, thanks.

No, prefiero no ver la película. = No, I'd prefer not to see the film.

Even more negatives...

There are more negatives you need to understand, and for top marks you should use them too.

not any more:	ya no
not anybody (nobody):	no ... nadie
not ever (never):	no ... nunca
not anything (nothing):	no ... nada
neither ... nor:	no ... ni ... ni
not any, not one:	no ... ningún/ninguna

Ya no voy a York. = I don't go to York any more.

No voy nunca a York. = I never go to York.

No voy ni a York ni a Belfast. = I don't go to York or to Belfast.

No hay nadie aquí. = There isn't anybody here.

Aquí no hay nada. = There isn't anything here.

No hay ningún plátano. = There aren't any bananas.

Just say no — and nobody and nothing and never...

Good news — it's nowhere near as bad as it looks. It seems confusing because you need 'no' with everything — but it actually makes life a lot easier when you're trying to spot negative sentences. Have a go at writing sentences using all the negative phrases here — it's the best way to learn 'em.

SUBJUNCTIVE

Subjunctive

OK, I'll admit it. This is tricky stuff. But it's very important if you want a top grade.

You have to use the present subjunctive in some situations

The present subjunctive isn't a new tense — it's just a different version of the present tense. It's used instead of the normal present tense in certain situations (see below).

To form the subjunctive, use the same stem as the 'I' form of the normal present tense, and then add the -ar present tense endings if it's an -er or -ir verb, or the -er endings if it's an -ar verb:

	HABLAR (hablo — I speak)	COMER (como — I eat)	VIVIR (vivo — I live)	TENER (tengo — I have)
I	hable	coma	viva	tenga
you (inf. sing.)	hables	comas	vivas	tengas
he/she/it/you (form. sing.)	hable	coma	viva	tenga
we	hablemos	comamos	vivamos	tengamos
you (inf. plu.)	habléis	comáis	viváis	tengáis
they/you (form. plu.)	hablen	coman	vivan	tengan

1. You use the subjunctive to get someone else to do something:

Elena quiere que Jorge lave los platos. = Elena wants Jorge to wash the dishes.

You don't need the subjunctive if only one person is involved, so 'Elena wants to wash the dishes' would be 'Elena quiere lavar los platos'.

2. After expressing an emotion or opinion about something :

Me alegro de que podáis venir a la fiesta. = I'm pleased that you can come to the party.

Stem changing verbs use the same vowel patterns as the present tense.

3. Expressing a wish or desire:

Espero que podamos volver a vernos pronto. = I hope we can see each other again soon.

4. Saying that something's unlikely to happen:

No creo que vaya a venir. = I don't think he's going to come.

'I think he is going to come' is 'creo que va a venir'.

These are irregular — 'vaya' is from 'ir' and 'sepa' is from 'saber'.

5. When there is a requirement:

Necesito a un amigo que sepa cocinar. = I need a friend who knows how to cook.

6. After 'cuando' (when), 'antes de que' (before) and 'aunque' (even if) if you're talking about the future:

Vamos a la playa mañana aunque llueva. = We're going to the beach tomorrow even if it rains.

7. After 'para que' (so that):

Vamos a un restaurante para que pruebes el gazpacho. = We're going to a restaurant so that you can try gazpacho.

You might see the imperfect subjunctive too

You don't need to be able to use the imperfect subjunctive, but you have to recognise it. The imperfect subjunctive isn't really used much in English, but the 'were' in 'if I were to win the lottery' is an example.

The imperfect subjunctive is formed using the stem (taken from the preterite) and adding these endings:

The one you'll see most often in Spanish is 'quisiera' (I would like), for polite requests.

	HABLAR	COMER	VIVIR
I	habl-ara	com-iera	viv-iera
you (informal sing.)	habl-aras	com-ieras	viv-ieras
he/she/it/you (formal sing.)	habl-ara	com-iera	viv-iera
nosotros/as	habl-áramos	com-iéramos	viv-iéramos
vosotros/as (informal plu.)	habl-arais	com-ierais	viv-ierais
they/you (formal plu.)	habl-aran	com-ieran	viv-ieran

You can't get someone else to learn this for you...

Shame. Oh well — there's only one thing for it and that's to learn everything on the page.

Ordering People Around

IMPERATIVE

Of course you need to understand this, and for top marks you need to be able to do it yourself too.

You need this stuff for bossing people about

Luckily, the singular informal (tú) bit is dead easy. It's just the same as the 'tú' part of the normal present tense, but without the 's' at the end.

hablas = you speak
¡Habla! = Speak!

bebes = you drink
¡Bebe! = Drink!

escribes = you write.
¡Escribe! = Write!

¡Escucha esto! = Listen to this!

There are a few common irregular ones:

decir	hacer	ir	oír	poner	salir	tener	venir
di	haz	ve	oye	pon	sal	ten	ven

To tell several people what to do in an informal way, take the infinitive and change the final 'r' to a 'd'.

hablar → ¡Hablad! salir → ¡Salid! hacer → ¡Haced! escribir → ¡Escribid! beber → ¡Bebed!

¡Terminad los deberes! = Finish your homework!

And for politely telling people what to do

To politely tell someone what to do, you use the formal 'you' part of the present subjunctive (see p. 106).

habla → ¡Hable! escribe → ¡Escriba!
come → ¡Coma! entra → ¡Entre!

The main exceptions are:

dar	haber	ir	saber	ser
dé	haya	vaya	sepa	sea

¡Siga todo recto. (seguir → siga)
= Continue straight on.

Coja la primera calle a la derecha. (coger → coja)
= Take the first street on the right.

At least the polite plural is easy — just add an 'n' as usual: ¡Hablen! ¡Coman! ¡Escriban! ¡Entren!

Put pronouns on the end of orders

With orders, pronouns (me, it, them, etc.) are stuck on the end:

¡Levántate! = Get up!

¡Tráigamelo! = Bring it to me!

Add 'no' for saying what not to do

For telling someone not to do something, you always use the subjunctive.

¡No escuches! = Don't listen!

You need to move any pronouns from the end to the beginning.

¡Tócalo! = Touch it!

¡No lo toques! = Don't touch it!

You're not the boss of me...

Brilliant — now you can order absolutely anyone around in Spanish. This stuff is dead handy.

'SABER', 'CONOCER' AND 'PODER'

'Know' and 'Can'

Here are three really useful verbs that people are always getting wrong — make sure you don't.

'To know information' is 'Saber'

1) Saber means 'to know', in the sense of having learnt something (like how to play the piano), or knowing information (like what time the bus leaves).

Have a look at these examples:

Ella sabe la respuesta a la pregunta.	She knows the answer to the question.
No sé si tenemos plátanos.	I don't know if we have any bananas.
¿Sabe usted cuándo llega el tren?	Do you know when the train arrives?

2) Saber followed by an infinitive means 'to know how to do something', in the sense of a skill, e.g.:

Sabe esquiar. = He/She knows how to ski.

No sabe leer. = He/She can't read.

Sé conducir. = I can drive.

IMPORTANT: 'saber' is a regular verb, except for the 'I' person, which is 'sé' (and the subjunctive, see p.106).

'To be familiar with' is 'Conocer'

Conocer means to know a person or place — to 'be familiar with'.
If someone asks you if you know their mate Gertrude, this is the one to use.

Conozco Madrid. = I know Madrid.

No conoce esta ciudad. = He/She doesn't know this town.

¿Conoces a mi amigo? = Do you know my friend?

You need the personal 'a' (see p. 92) when talking about knowing people.

IMPORTANT: like 'saber', 'conocer' is also a normal verb with an odd 'I' person = 'conozco'.

'Poder' means 'to be able to'

Poder (to be able to / can) has three very important meanings:

1) Being able to do something (not knowing how to do it, but just being able to — like 'Yes, I can come tomorrow').

Si quieres, puedo llevar el equipaje. = I can carry the luggage if you like.

2) Permission to do something. *Se pueden sacar fotos aquí.* = You can take photos here.

3) Possibility — something could be the case. *Eso puede pasar.* = That can happen.

But can you can-can...

Three mega-handy verbs that you need to sort out. Don't forget the difference between saber and conocer, and make sure that you know the three meanings of poder. Wonderful stuff...

'How Long', '-ing' & 'Just Done'

Pluperfect Tense, Present Participles & Acabar De

Three more bits to learn — you may come across them in the listening or reading papers.

¿Cuánto tiempo hace que...? — How long...?

To ask how long someone's been doing something, use '¿Cuánto tiempo hace que...' followed by a verb in the present tense.

¿Cuánto tiempo hace que aprendes español? = How long have you been learning Spanish?

To say how long you've been doing something, say what you've been doing in the present tense, followed by 'desde hace' and the length of time you've been doing it for.

Aprendo español desde hace tres años. = I've been learning Spanish for three years.

Remember to use the present tense — you don't say 'I have been' like in English.

Use the imperfect with 'desde hacía' to say what you had been doing.

Aprendía español desde hacía tres años. = I had been learning Spanish for three years.

Use present participles to say what you're doing right now

Most of the time you'd translate things like 'I am doing' and 'I was doing' with normal tenses — those two would be 'hago' (present tense), and 'hacía' (imperfect tense).

But sometimes you want to stress that something is happening at the moment, or was happening in the past.

e.g.: *Estoy almorzando.* = I'm having my lunch.

Estaba durmiendo cuando sonó el teléfono. = He/She was sleeping when the phone rang.

There are two bits to this:

a) the correct part of 'estar' (to be) in the present or the imperfect tense, and

b) the special word for the 'ing' bit — called the present participle.

'-ar' verbs e.g. hablar	'-er' verbs e.g. comer	'-ir' verbs e.g. vivir
stem (e.g. habl) + ando	stem (e.g. com) + iendo	stem (e.g. viv) + iendo
hablando	comiendo	viviendo

There are only a few irregular ones you need to know:

- caer → cayendo
- servir → sirviendo
- dormir → durmiendo
- seguir → siguiendo
- leer → leyendo
- pedir → pidiendo
- morir → muriendo

Acabo de... — 'I have just...'

To say what's just happened, use the present tense of 'acabar' + 'de' + the verb you want in the infinitive.

I:	acabo	we:	acabamos
you (inf.sing.):	acabas	you (inf.plu.):	acabáis
he / she / it / you (form.sing.):	acaba	they / you (form.plu.):	acaban

Acabo de ducharme. = I have just taken a shower.

Acaba de salir. = She has just left.

The end of grammar — you deserve a medal...

Phew. Just the revision questions on the next page to go now, and then you're done — hurray.

REVISION SUMMARY

Revision Summary

Hurray! Hurray! It's the end of the book! Hurray! Hurray! Before you get too carried away, do all these lovely revision questions. You know the drill by now — do the questions without looking back at the pages, and if there are any you can't do, go back over those pages and revise them (or re-revise them, or re-re-revise them, or whatever) until you know it all forwards, backwards, standing on your head and doing cartwheels. One more time, here we go...

1) What are all the Spanish words for a) a b) the?
2) How do you say the following in Spanish?
   a) the big dog b) the small cat c) the small dogs d) the black cats
3) What's the difference between these two phrases in Spanish?
   a) Pablo es un gran hombre. b) Pablo es un hombre grande.
4) What do these endings do to adjectives? a) ito b) ísimo
5) How do you say these in Spanish? a) my flower b) his flower c) our flower
6) Meg asks Ben "¿Esas gafas de sol son tuyas?", and he replies "No, las mías son azules." Write out their conversation in English.
7) 'Tranquilo' means 'calm' in Spanish — how would you say 'calmly'?
8) How do you say 'I sing well' in Spanish? How about 'I sing very badly'?
9) How would you say these in Spanish? a) Helen is the tallest b) this song is the best
10) What does 'Ricardo es el que baila mejor' mean?
11) How would you say 'the cheese is more expensive than the milk' in Spanish? How about 'the cheese is as expensive as the milk'?
12) What do these joining words mean? a) o b) porque c) pero d) si
13) What do these little words mean? a) de b) sobre c) a d) en e) detrás de
14) Give three situations where you would use 'por', and three where you would use 'para'.
15) 'Jane compra la falda' means 'Jane buys the skirt'. How would you say 'Jane buys it?' Jane is buying the skirt for her mum — how would you say 'Jane buys it for her'?
16) How do you say 'Do you want to come with me?' in Spanish?
17) Say whether these sentences are right or wrong:
   a) Estoy buscando a una tienda. b) Estoy buscando a mi hermano.
   c) Estoy buscando Susana. d) Tengo dos hermanas.
18) How do you say 'this house' in Spanish? What about 'that house'? And 'that house over there'?
19) What does 'Alguien está en la casa' mean?
20) How do you say these in Spanish? a) you live b) he talks c) we eat
21) What is the 'I' form of these verbs? a) pensar b) tener c) sentarse d) preferir
22) Write out two sentences with 'ser', and two with 'estar'.
23) What does 'Iré a la playa' mean? What's another way of saying this in Spanish?
24) How do you say these in Spanish? a) I would dance b) they would dance
25) What's the past participle of these verbs? a) abrir b) hablar c) tener d) decir
26) What do these mean? a) he ido b) habéis ido c) han ido d) has ido
27) How do you say 'I ate a burger' in Spanish? How about 'he ate a burger'?
28) What do these mean? a) tuvo b) dijo c) dieron d) pusiste
29) How do you say 'I used to go to the beach every summer' in Spanish?
30) 'Lavarse' is 'to get washed' in Spanish. How do you say 'I get washed'? What about 'they get washed'? And 'you (sing.) don't get washed'?
31) Write out all the forms of the present subjunctive for 'hablar'.
32) How do you say 'Speak!' a) politely to one person b) informally to a group?
33) Translate these phrases: a) I know how to swim. b) I know Jenny. c) Can you repeat it?
34) What does 'estoy comiendo' mean?
35) How do you say 'he has just left' in Spanish?

Do Well in Your Exam

Here are some little gems of advice, whichever exam board you're studying for.

Read the Questions carefully

Don't go losing easy marks — it'll break my heart. Make sure you definitely do the things on this list in the listening and reading exams:

1) Read all the instructions properly.
2) Read the question properly.
3) Answer the question — don't waffle.
4) Use the time to plan your answers.

Don't give up if you don't Understand

If you don't understand, don't panic. The key thing to remember is that you can still do well in the exam, even if you don't understand every Spanish word that comes up. Look at the words and see if there are any that seem familiar:

If you're reading or listening — look for lookalikes

1) Some words look or sound the same in Spanish and English — they're called cognates.
2) These words are great because you'll recognise them when you see them in a text.
3) Be careful though — there are some exceptions you need to watch out for. Some words look like an English word but have a totally different meaning:

la nota:	*mark*	el pariente:	*relative*	sensible:	*sensitive*
el pie:	*foot*	la sopa:	*soup*	largo:	*long*
el campo:	*countryside*	el éxito:	*success*	actual:	*present*
la carpeta:	*file, folder*	la ropa:	*clothes*	fatal:	*awful*
la dirección:	*address*	la librería:	*bookshop*	embarazada:	*pregnant*

Words like these are called 'falsos amigos' — false friends.

Make use of the Context

You're likely to come across the odd word that you don't know, especially in the reading exam. Often you'll be able to find some clues telling you what the text is all about.

1) The type of text, e.g. newspaper article, advertisement, website
2) The title of the text
3) Any pictures
4) The verbal context

Say you see the following in the reading exam, and don't know what any of these words mean:

"...ropa hecha de poliéster, de lana, de cuero y de nylon."

1) Well, the fact that this is a list of things, all starting with 'de' coming after the Spanish word for 'clothes' suggests they're all things that clothes can be made out of.
2) You can guess that 'poliéster' means 'polyester', and 'nylon' means 'nylon'. Obviously.
3) So it's a pretty good guess that the two words you don't know are different types of fabric. (In fact, 'lana' means 'wool' and 'cuero' means 'leather'.)
4) Often the questions won't depend on you understanding these more difficult words. It's important to be able to understand the gist though, and not let these words throw you.

Exams are important — failing can be fatal...

Don't get caught out by words that look like English words, but in fact mean something different. Generally speaking, if a word doesn't seem to fit into the context of the question, have a re-think.

Do Well in Your Exam

These pages could improve your grade — they're all about exam technique. No learning in sight...

Look at how a word is made up

You may read or hear a sentence and not understand how the sentence works. You need to remember all the grammary bits in Section 7 to give you a good chance at piecing it all together.

1) A word that ends in '-ado' or '-ido' may well be a past participle (see p. 100). Look for a bit of 'haber' nearby to work out who's done what.

2) A word that ends in '-ar', '-er' or '-ir' might be an infinitive. If you take off the last two letters it might look like an English word which may tell you what the verb means.

   e.g. 'confirm~~ar~~' = to confirm

3) If you see '-mente' at the end of a word, it could well be an adverb (see p. 86). Try replacing the '-mente' with '-ly' and see if it makes sense.

   e.g. 'especial~~mente~~' = especially

4) When a word ends in '-dad', it's often replaced with '-ty' in English.

   e.g. 'socie~~dad~~' = society

5) Don't forget to look at the beginning of the word too. There is sometimes a sneaky 'e-' added to the start of a few nouns that begin with an 's-' in English.

   e.g. 'estéreo' = stereo 'estación' = station

6) A word beginning with 'in-' or 'des-' might be a negative prefix.

   e.g. 'inútil' = 'in+útil' = useless

A prefix is a part of a word that comes before the main bit of the word.

Take notes in the listening exam

1) You'll have 5 minutes at the start of the exam to have a quick look through the paper. This'll give you a chance to see how many questions there are, and you might get a few clues from the questions about what topics they're on, so it won't be a horrible surprise when the CD starts playing.
2) You'll hear each extract twice. Different people have different strategies, but it's a good idea to jot down a few details that you think might come up in the questions, especially things like:
3) But... don't forget to keep listening to the gist of the recording while you're making notes.
4) You won't have a dictionary — but you probably wouldn't have time to use it anyway.

Dates
Numbers
Spelled-out names

Estop trying to escare me about estupid exams...

The examiners aren't above sticking a few tricky bits and pieces into the exam to see how you cope with them. Using all your expert knowledge, you should stand a pretty good chance of working it out. And if you can't make an educated guess, make an uneducated guess... but try something.

How To Use Dictionaries

Don't go mad on dictionaries — it's the path to ruin. However, you're allowed to use one in the writing tasks and to prepare for the speaking task, so it's good idea to make the most of it.

Don't translate Word for Word — it DOESN'T work

If you turn each word of this phrase into English, you get rubbish.

Me gusta nadar. ✗→ *Me it pleases to swim.*

It's the same the other way round — turn English into Spanish word by word, and you get balderdash — don't do it.

I have finished. ✗→ *Tengo terminado.* NO!

If it Doesn't make Sense, you've got it Wrong

Some words have several meanings — don't just pick the first one you see. Look at the meanings listed and suss out which one is what you're looking for.

If you read this... *Me duele el ojo derecho.*

...you might look up 'derecho' and find this:

> **derecho, a**
> adj straight; upright;
> // right, right-hand
> // adv straight // nm law; justice
> tener derecho a hacer algo: to have the right to do something
> derecho de paso: right of way
> // derechos; rights; taxes; duties

So the sentence could mean:

My straight eye hurts. ✗

My right eye hurts. ✔

My law eye hurts. ✗

This is the only one that sounds sensible.

Verbs change according to the person

When you look up a verb in the dictionary, you'll find the infinitive (the 'to' form, like 'to run', 'to sing' etc.). But you may need to say 'I run', or 'we sing' — so you need to change the verb ending.

Say you need to say 'I buy'.

1) If you looked up 'buy', you'd find the word 'comprar', meaning 'to buy'.
2) But 'comprar' is the infinitive — you can't put 'yo comprar'.
3) You need the 'I' (yo) form of the verb — 'compro'.
4) Check the tense too — e.g. you don't want 'compré'.

For the lowdown on verbs and all their different endings, see the grammar section.

If you're looking up a Spanish verb, look for its infinitive (it'll end in 'ar', 'er' or 'ir'). If you want to know what 'tocamos' means, you'll find 'tocar' (to touch, or to play) in the dictionary. So 'tocamos' must mean 'we touch' or 'we play', depending on the context.

Dictionaries — useful for holding doors open*...

Don't get put off dictionaries by this page. They're lovely really. Just make sure your writing technique isn't to look up every single word and then bung them down in order. Cos it'll be rubbish.

* No. 37 from a list of '101 great uses for your dictionary'.

Hints for Writing

Here are a few general hints about how you should approach the writing tasks.

Write about what you know

1) You won't be asked to write about nineteenth century Spanish novelists.
2) You will need to cover certain specific things that the question asks you to, but there'll be plenty of scope to be imaginative.
3) Usually the writing tasks will give you some flexibility so you can base your answer on something you know about.

No sé nada...

You need to say When and Why...

1) Saying when and how often you did things gets you big bonus marks. Learn times, dates and numbers carefully (p. 1–3).
2) Make sure you talk about what you've done in the past (see p. 100–103) or what you will do in the future (p. 98).
3) Give descriptions where possible, but keep things accurate — a short description in perfect Spanish is better than a longer paragraph of nonsense.
4) Examiners also love opinions (p. 7–8). Try to vary them as much as possible.

So, if I add one more drop we'll go back in time two hours...

...two hours later...

...and Where and Who With...

Examiners really are quite nosy, and love as many details as you can give. It's a good idea to ask yourself all these 'wh-' questions, and write the bits that show your Spanish off in the best light. Also, it doesn't matter if what you're writing is strictly true or not — as long as it's believable.

Use your dictionary, but sparingly

1) The time to use the dictionary is NOT to learn a completely new, fancy way of saying something.
2) Use it to look up a particular word that you've forgotten — a word that, when you see it, you'll know it's the right word.
3) Use it to check genders of nouns — that's whether words are masculine (el/un) or feminine (la/una).
4) Check any spellings you're unsure of.

Most importantly, don't use the dictionary to delve into the unknown. If you don't know what you've written is right, it's probably wrong.

Take your time

1) Don't hurtle into writing about something and then realise half-way through that you don't actually know the Spanish for it.
2) Plan how you can cover all the things that the task mentions, and then think about the extra things you can slip in to show off your Spanish.

Take me.

And lastly, don't forget your pen...

I suppose the key is variety — lots of different tenses, plenty of meaty vocabulary and loads of details. This is your only chance to show what you can do, so don't waste all your hard work.

Hints for Writing

Accuracy is really important in the writing assessment. Without it, your work will look like sloppy custard.

Start with the Verb

Verbs are doing words. See p. 94.

1) Verbs really are the cornerstone of every Spanish sentence.
   If you get the verb right, the rest of the sentence should fall into place.
2) Be careful that you get the whole expression that uses the verb, not just the verb itself.

EXAMPLE: Say you want to write the following sentence in Spanish:

If I am in a hurry, I take the bus to school.

Don't see 'I am' and jump in with 'ser' or 'estar'. The expression for 'to be in a hurry' is 'tener prisa'.

You know that 'to take the bus' is 'coger el autobús'.

Make sure your tenses and the endings of the verbs are right, then piece it all together:

Si tengo prisa, cojo el autobús para ir al instituto.

Check and re-check

No matter how careful you think you're being, mistakes can easily creep into your work.
Go through the check-list below for every sentence straight after you've written it.

1) Are the verbs in the right TENSE?
   Ayer, juego al fútbol en el parque. ✗ — Ayer, jugué al fútbol en el parque. ✓
2) Are the ENDINGS of the verbs right?
   Mi hermano no quieren salir. ✗ — Mi hermano no quiere salir. ✓
3) Do your adjectives AGREE as they should?
   La profesora es alto. ✗ — La profesora es alta. ✓
4) Do your reflexive verbs and pronouns AGREE?
   A las siete, me levantamos. ✗ — A las siete, me levanto. ✓
5) Do your adjectives come in the RIGHT PLACE?
   Una blanca falda ✗ — Una falda blanca. ✓
6) Have you used USTED/USTEDES correctly?
   Señor, puedes ayudarme, por favor? ✗ — Señor, puede usted ayudarme, por favor? ✓

Then when you've finished the whole piece of work, have another read through with fresh eyes.
You're bound to pick up one or two more mistakes.

Do nothing without a verb...

I know there's loads to remember, and Spanish verbs are a pain, but checking over your work is a real must. Re-read your work assuming there are errors in it, rather than assuming it's fine as it is.

Hints for Speaking

The speaking assessment fills many a student with dread. Remember though — it's your chance to show what you can do. It won't be nearly as bad as you think it's going to be. Honest.

Be Imaginative

There are two tricky things about the speaking assessment — one is what to say, and two is how to say it. No matter how good your Spanish is, it won't shine through if you can't think of anything to say.

Say you're talking about your daily routine (or to imagine someone else's daily routine). It would be easy to give a list of things you do when you get in from school:

"Hago mis deberes. Veo la televisión. Como la cena. Me acuesto."

= I do my homework. I watch television. I eat dinner. I go to bed.

It makes sense, but the problem is, it's all a bit samey...

1) Try to think of when this isn't the case, and put it into a DIFFERENT TENSE:

"Pero mañana, será diferente, porque voy a jugar al hockey después del instituto."

= But tomorrow, it will be different, because I'm going to play hockey after school.

2) Don't just talk about yourself. Talk about OTHER PEOPLE — even if you have to imagine them.

"Vi la televisión con mi hermano, pero no nos gustan los mismos programas."

= I watched television with my brother, but we don't like the same programmes.

3) Give loads of OPINIONS and REASONS for your opinions.

"Me gusta hacer ejercicio antes de comer. Luego puedo relajarme más tarde."

= I like to do exercise before eating. Then I can relax later on.

A couple of 'DON'T's...

1) DON'T try to avoid a topic if you find it difficult — that'll mean you won't get any marks at all for that bit of the assessment. You'll be surprised what you can muster up if you stay calm and concentrate on what you do know how to say.
2) DON'T make up a word in the hope that it exists in Spanish unless you're really, really stuck and you've tried all the other tricks on this page. If it's your last resort, it's worth a try.

Have Confidence

1) Believe it or not, your teacher isn't trying to catch you out. He or she wants you to do well, and wants to be dazzled by all the excellent Spanish you've learnt.
2) Speaking assessments can be pretty daunting. But remember it's the same for everyone.
3) Nothing horrendous is going to happen if you make a few slip-ups. Just try and focus on showing your teacher how much you've learnt.

Imagine there's no speaking assessment...

It's easy if you try. But that's not going to get you a GCSE. The main thing to remember is that it's much better to have too much to say than too little. Bear in mind the 3 ways to make your answers more imaginative. This will give you an opportunity to show off your beautiful Spanish.

Hints for Speaking

Nothing in life ever goes completely according to plan. So it's a good idea to prepare yourself for a few hiccups in the speaking assessment. (Nothing to do with glasses of water.)

Try to find another way of saying it

There may be a particular word or phrase that trips you up. There's always a way round it though.

1) If you can't remember a Spanish word, use an alternative word or try describing it instead.
2) For example, if you can't remember that 'grapes' are 'las uvas' and you really need to say it, then describe them as 'the small green or red fruits', or 'las frutas pequeñas que son verdes o rojas'.
3) You can fib to avoid words you can't remember — if you can't remember the word for 'dog' then just say you've got a cat instead. Make sure what you're saying makes sense though — saying you've got a pet radio isn't going to get you any marks, trust me.
4) If you can't remember the word for a cup (una taza) in your speaking assessment, you could say a 'glass' (un vaso) instead — you'll still make yourself understood.

If the worst comes to the worst, ask for help in Spanish

1) If you can't think of a way around it, you can ask for help in the speaking assessment — as long as you ask for it in Spanish.
2) If you can't remember what a chair is, ask your teacher: "¿Cómo se dice 'chair' en español?" It's better than wasting time trying to think of the word.

You may just need to buy yourself some time

If you get a bit stuck for what to say, there's always a way out.

1) If you just need some thinking time in your speaking assessment or you want to check something, you can use these useful sentences to help you out:

Este...	*Um...*	¿Puede repetir, por favor?	*Can you repeat, please?*
Pues...	*Well...*	No entiendo.	*I don't understand.*
No estoy seguro/a.	*I'm not sure.*	Esa es una buena pregunta.	*That's a good question.*

2) Another good tactic if you're a bit stuck is to say what you've just said in a different way. This shows off your command of Spanish, and also it might lead onto something else, e.g.:

Comemos juntos. No como solo, excepto cuando mis padres trabajan hasta tarde.

Saying the same thing a different way... leading on to another idea.

We eat together. I don't eat on my own, except when my parents work late.

And don't be afraid to make mistakes — even native Spanish speakers make 'em. Don't let a silly error shake your concentration for the rest of the assessment.

One last thing — don't panic...

Congratulations — you've made it to the end of the book. And without accident or injury, I hope — paper cuts hurt more than people think... Anyway, enough of this idle chit-chat. Read these pages, take on board the information, use it in your GCSE, do well and then celebrate in style.

A

a prep *at, to*
a diario ad *daily*
a eso de prep *at around*
a fines de prep *at the end of*
a la plancha a *grilled*
a mediados de prep *in the middle of*
a menudo ad *often*
a mitad de precio a *half-price*
a partir de prep *from*
a pesar de prep *in spite of*
a pie ad *on foot*
¿A qué hora? *What time?*
a tiempo ad *in time*
a tiempo completo a *full-time*
a tiempo parcial a *part-time*
a un paso (de) prep *a short distance (from)*
a veces ad *sometimes*
abajo ad *down, downstairs, below*
el abanico m *fan*
abierto a *open*
el/la abogado/a mf *lawyer*
el abrigo m *overcoat*
abril m *April*
abrir v *to open*
la abuela f *grandmother*
el abuelo m *grandfather*
aburrido a *bored, boring*
aburrirse vr *to be/get bored*
acabar v *to finish, end*
acabar de v *to have just… (done something)*
acampar v *to camp*
acceder a v *to access (e.g. the internet)*
el acceso m *access, entrance*
el accidente m *accident*
el aceite m *oil*
la aceituna f *olive*
el acento m *accent*
aceptable a *acceptable*
aceptar v *to accept*
acoger v *to receive*
acompañar v *to accompany*
aconsejar v *to advise*
acordarse (de) vr *to remember*
el acoso escolar m *bullying*
acostarse vr *to go to bed*
la actividad f *activity*
activo a *active*
el actor m *actor*
la actriz f *actress*
la actuación f *performance*
actuar v *to act*
adelante ad *forward*
además ad *in addition*
adictivo a *addictive*
el adicto m *addict*
¡Adiós! interj *goodbye*
adjuntar v *to attach*
admirar v *to admire*
adolescente a *adolescent*
el adolescente m *teenager*
¿Adónde? ad *Where?*
adoptar v *to adopt*
adoptivo a *adopted*
adorar v *to adore/worship*
la aduana f *customs*
el/la adulto/a mf *adult*
advertir v *to warn/tell*
el aeropuerto m *airport*
afectar v *to affect*
la afición f *hobby*
el/la aficionado/a mf *fan*
afortunado a *lucky*
afuera (de) ad *outside*
las afueras fpl *outskirts*
la agencia de viajes f *travel agency*
el/la agente inmobiliario/a mf *estate agent*
agosto m *August*
agotar v *to exhaust*
agradable a *pleasant*
agradecer v *to thank*
agresivo a *aggressive*
el agua f *water*
el agua mineral (con/sin gas) f *mineral water (sparkling/still)*
aguantar v *to put up with, stand*
el agujero m *hole*
ahí ad *there*
ahora ad *now*
ahorrar v *to save*
el aire m *air*
el aire acondicionado m *air conditioning*
aislado a *isolated*
el ajedrez m *chess*
el ajo m *garlic*
al aire libre a *outdoor*
al aparato interj *speaking (answering the telephone)*
al final (de) prep *in the end/at the end (of)*
al lado de prep *next to*
al mismo tiempo ad *at the same time*
el albañil m *bricklayer*
el albergue juvenil m *youth hostel*
alcanzar v *to reach*
el/la alcohólico/a mf *alcoholic*
el alcoholismo m *alcoholism*
la aldea f *village/hamlet*
alegrarse vr *to be happy*
alegre a *happy*
alemán a *German*
el/la alemán/ana mf *German man/woman*
Alemania f *Germany*
la alfombra f *carpet*
algo pron *something*
el algodón m *cotton*
alguien pron *someone*
algunas veces ad *sometimes*
algún/alguno/alguna a *any*
la alimentación f *food, nutrition*
el alimento m *food*
allá ad *there*
allí ad *there*
almorzar v *to eat lunch*
el alojamiento m *accommodation*
alojarse vr *to stay, to lodge*
el alpinismo m *mountain climbing*
alquilado a *rented*
alquilar v *to rent, to hire*
el alquiler m *rent*
el alquiler de coches m *car hire*
alrededor (de) ad *around, about*
alto a *high, tall*
la altura f *height*
el/la alumno/a mf *pupil*
el ama de casa f *housewife*
amable a *kind*
amarillo a *yellow*
la ambición f *ambition*
ambicioso a *ambitious*
ambiente m *atmosphere*
amenazar v *to threaten*
América del Sur f *South America*
el/la amigo/a mf *friend*
el/la amigo/a por correspondencia mf *penfriend*
amistoso a *friendly*
el amor m *love*
ancho a *wide*
anciano a *old*
el/la anciano/a mf *old man/woman*
Andalucía f *Andalusia*
andar v *to walk*
el andén m *platform*
el anillo m *ring*
animado a *lively, animated*
el animal doméstico m *pet*
el aniversario m *anniversary*
anoche ad *last night*
anteayer ad *the day before yesterday*
antes (de) ad *before*
antiguo a *old, antique*
antipático a *unpleasant*
anular v *to cancel*
el anuncio m *advert*
añadir v *to add*
el año m *year*
el Año Nuevo m *New Year*
apagar v *to turn out, to put out, to switch off*
el aparcamiento m *car park*
aparcar v *to park*
el apartamento m *flat*
aparte de ad *apart from*
el apellido m *surname*
apetecer v *to feel like*
el apodo m *nickname*
el apoyo m *support*
apoyar v *to lean, to support*
apreciar v *to like, to value*
aprender (a) v *to learn (to)*
el/la aprendiz mf *apprentice*
aprobar v *to pass (exam)*
apropiado a *suitable*
aprovecharse (de) vr *to take advantage*
aproximadamente ad *approximately*
apto a *suitable, capable*
los apuntes mpl *notes*
aquel a *that*
aquí ad *here*
Aragón f *Aragon*
el árbol m *tree*
el archivo m *file*
Argentina f *Argentina*
argentino a *Argentinian*
el armario m *cupboard, wardrobe*
arreglar v *to arrange/repair*
arreglarse vr *to get ready*
arrepentirse vr *to be sorry, regret*
arriba ad *upstairs, up*
arriba de prep *above*
la arroba f *@*
el arroz m *rice*
arruinar v *to ruin*
el arte dramático m *drama, theatre*
el artículo m *article*
el/la artista mf *artist*
asado a *roast*
el ascensor m *lift*
los aseos mpl *toilets*
así así a *so-so*
así que conj *so*
el asiento m *seat*
la asignatura f *school subject*
el aspecto m *aspect, appearance*
atacar v *to attack*
el ataque cardíaco m *heart attack*
el atasco m *traffic jam*
la atención f *attention*
atentamente ad *sincerely*
atento a *attentive*
el ático m *attic*
el/la atleta mf *athlete*
el atletismo m *athletics*
la atmósfera f *atmosphere*
atractivo a *attractive*
atrás ad *behind*
atrevido a *daring*
el atún m *tuna fish*
el aula f *classroom, lecture room*
aumentar v *to increase*
el aumento m *increase*
aun (si) conj *even (if)*
aunque conj *although*
ausente a *absent*
Austria f *Austria*
austríaco a *Austrian*
el autobús m *bus*
el autocar m *coach*
la autopista f *motorway*
el auxiliar de vuelo m *flight attendant (male)*
avaro a *mean/stingy*
el AVE m *high-speed train service*
la avería f *breakdown*
averiado a *broken down*
el avión m *aeroplane*
el aviso m *notice, warning*
ayer ad *yesterday*
la ayuda f *help*
ayudar v *to help*
el ayuntamiento m *town hall*
la azafata f *air hostess*
el azúcar m *sugar*
azul a *blue*

B

el bacalao m *cod*
el bachillerato m *higher certificate (A level)*
el bádminton m *badminton*
bailar v *to dance*
el baile m *dance*
bajar v *to take/go down*
bajo a *low, short*
bajo prep *below*
el balcón m *balcony*
el balón m *ball*
el baloncesto m *basketball*
el banco m *bank*
la bandeja f *tray*
la banda ancha f *broadband*
el bañador m *swimming costume*
bañar(se) vr *to bathe*
la bañera f *bathtub*
el baño m *bath, bathroom*
barato a *cheap*
la barba f *beard*
el barco m *boat, ship*
la barra (de pan) f *loaf (of bread)*
la barrera generacional f *generation gap*
el barrio m *district, neighbourhood*
¡Basta! interj *That's enough!*
bastante a/ad *enough, quite a lot*
bastar v *to be enough*
la basura f *rubbish*
la batería f *drums*
el bebé m *baby*
beber v *to drink*
la bebida f *drink*
beige a *beige*
Bélgica f *Belgium*
beneficiar v *to benefit*
el beneficio m *benefit*
besar v *to kiss*
el beso m *kiss*
la biblioteca f *library*
la bicicleta/bici f *bicycle/bike*
bien ad *well/good*
bien educado a *well mannered*
bien hecho a *well done*
¡Bienvenido/a! interj *Welcome!*

el bigote m *moustache*
el billar m *snooker*
el billete m *ticket/banknote*
el billete de ida / el billete sencillo m *single ticket*
el billete de ida y vuelta m *return ticket*
la biología f *biology*
el bistec/bisté m *steak*
blanco a *white*
el blog m *blog*
el bloque m *block*
la blusa f *blouse*
la boca f *mouth*
el bocadillo m *sandwich*
la boda f *wedding*
la bolera f *bowling alley*
el bolígrafo/el boli m *ballpoint pen*
la bolsa de plástico f *carrier bag*
el bolso m *bag, handbag*
el bombero m *fireman*
el bombón m *chocolate, sweet*
bonito a *pretty, nice*
el bonobús m *bus pass*
borracho a *drunk*
el borrador m *(board) rubber*
borrar v *to rub out, delete*
el bosque m *wood*
la bota f *boot*
el bote m *boat*
la botella f *bottle*
el botón m *button*
el boxeo m *boxing*
el brazo m *arm*
breve a *brief*
británico a *British*
broncearse vr *to get a suntan, sunbathe*
buen/mal tiempo m *good/bad weather*
¡Buen viaje! *Have a good trip!*
¡Buena suerte! *Good luck!*
Buenas noches interj *Good night*
Buenas tardes interj *Good afternoon/evening*
bueno a *good*
Buenos días interj *Good day/Hello*
la bufanda f *scarf*
buscar v *to look for, fetch*
la butaca f *armchair, seat (in cinema, theatre)*
el buzón m *post box*

C

c/ (= calle) f *street*
el caballo m *horse*
la cabeza f *head*
cada a *each, every*
caerse vr *to fall, fall over*
el café m *coffee*
el café con leche m *white coffee*
la cafetería f *coffee shop/café*
la caja f *box, till*
el/la cajero/a mf *cashier*
los calamares mpl *squid*
los calcetines mpl *socks*
la calculadora f *calculator*
la calefacción f *heating*
el calentamiento m *warming*
la calidad f *quality*
caliente a *hot*
la calificación f *grade, mark*
calificado a *qualified*
callado a *quiet/silent*
callar(se) v(r) *to say nothing*
la calle f *street*
el calor m *heat*
caluroso a *warm, hot*
calvo a *bald*
calzar v *to wear (shoes)*
la cama f *bed*
la cama de matrimonio f *double bed*
la cámara f *camera*
el/la camarero/a mf *waiter/waitress*
cambiar v *to change*
el cambio m *change, bureau de change*
caminar v *to walk*
el camino m *road, track, route*
el camión m *lorry*
el/la camionero/a mf *lorry driver*
la camisa f *shirt*
la camiseta f *T-shirt*
el camisón m *nightdress*
la campaña f *campaign*
el/la campeón/a mf *champion*
el campeonato m *championship*
el camping m *campsite*
el campo m *field, country*
el campo de deportes / el campo deportivo m *sports field*
las (Islas) Canarias fpl *Canary Islands*
el canario m *canary*
la cancha (de tenis) f *(tennis) court*
la canción f *song*
el candidato m *candidate*
cansado a *tired*
cansar v *to tire*
el/la cantante mf *singer*
cantar v *to sing*
la cantidad f *quantity*
la cantina f *canteen*
la capa de ozono f *ozone layer*
la cara f *face*
el carácter m *character/personality*
el caramelo m *sweet*
la caravana f *caravan*
la cárcel f *prison*
cargar v *to load/charge*
el cariño m *affection*
cariñoso a *affectionate*
la carne f *meat*
el carnet m *pass*
el carnet de identidad m *ID card*
el carnet de conducir m *driving licence*
la carnicería f *butcher's*
el/la carnicero/a mf *butcher*
caro a *expensive*
la carpeta f *folder, file*
el carpintero m *carpenter*
la carrera f *race/profession*
la carretera f *road*
la carta f *letter, menu*
las cartas fpl *playing cards*
el/la cartero/a mf *postman/postwoman*
el cartón m *cardboard/carton*
la casa f *house*
la casa adosada f *semi-detached house*
casado a *married*
el casamiento m *marriage, wedding*
casarse vr *to get married*
el casco m *helmet*
casi ad *almost*
castaño a *chestnut brown*
las castañuelas fpl *castanets*
castellano a *Spanish, Castilian*
castigar v *to punish*
el castigo m *punishment*
Castilla f *Castille*
el castillo m *castle*
Cataluña f *Catalonia*
la catedral f *cathedral*
causar v *to cause*
la cazadora f *jacket*
el CD m *CD*
la cebolla f *onion*
celebrar v *to celebrate*
celoso a *jealous*
la cena f *dinner, evening meal*
cenar v *to have dinner*
el centímetro m *centimetre*
el céntimo m *cent*
céntrico a *central*
el centro m *centre*
en el centro de prep *in the centre of*
el centro comercial m *shopping centre*
el cepillo m *brush*
la cerámica f *ceramics/pottery*
cerca (de) ad/prep *near (to)*
los cereales mpl *cereal*
el cerebro m *brain*
cerrado a *closed*
cerrar v *to shut*
la cerveza f *beer*
el césped m *lawn*
los CFC mpl *CFCs*
el chalet/chalé m *detached house*
los champiñones mpl *mushrooms*
el chándal m *tracksuit*
la chaqueta f *jacket*
la charcutería f *delicatessen*
charlar v *to chat*
chatear v *to chat (online)*
el cheque m *cheque*
el cheque de viaje m *traveller's cheque*
la chica f *girl*
el chicle m *chewing gum*
el chico m *boy*
Chile f *Chile*
chileno a *Chilean*
la chimenea f *chimney, fireplace*
el chocolate m *chocolate/hot chocolate*
el chorizo m *spicy pork sausage*
el chubasco m *heavy shower*
la chuleta f *chop, cutlet*
los churros mpl *flour fritters*
el cibercafé m *cybercafe*
el ciberespacio m *cyberspace*
el ciclismo m *cycling*
el cielo m *sky, heaven*
la ciencia ficción f *science fiction*
las ciencias fpl *science*
las ciencias económicas fpl *economics*
cierto a *true, certain, sure*
la cifra f *figure, digit*
el cigarrillo m *cigarette*
el cine m *cinema*
el cinturón m *belt*
el cinturón de seguridad m *seat belt*
la cita f *appointment, date*
la ciudad f *city, large town*
el clarinete m *clarinet*
claro a *clear, obvious, light (coloured)*
claro que ad *of course...*
¡Claro! interj *Of course!*
la clase f *class, lesson*
clásico a *classical*
el/la cliente mf *customer, client*
el clima m *climate*
la clínica f *clinic*
el club m *club*
el club de jóvenes m *youth club*
cobarde a *cowardly*
la cobaya f *guinea pig*
cobrar v *to charge*
la cocaína f *cocaine*
el coche m *car*
la cocina (de gas/eléctrica) f *(gas/electric) oven*
la cocina f *kitchen, cookery, food technology*
cocinar v *to cook*
el/la cocinero/a mf *cook*
el código postal m *postcode*
coger v *to take, pick, catch*
la col f *cabbage*
la colección f *collection*
coleccionar v *to collect*
el colegio m *school, college*
la coliflor f *cauliflower*
el collar m *necklace*
Colombia f *Colombia*
colombiano a *Colombian*
el color m *colour*
el combustible (fósil) m *(fossil) fuel*
la comedia f *comedy, play*
el comedor m *dining room*
comenzar v *to begin*
comer v *to eat*
el/la comerciante mf *shopkeeper*
el comercio m *business studies/commerce/shop*
cometer v *to commit*
cómico a *funny*
la comida f *food, meal, lunch*
la comida basura f *junk food*
la comida rápida f *fast food*
el comienzo m *start*
la comisaría f *police station*
como ad *how, like, as, about*
¿Cómo? interj *Pardon?*
¿Cómo está(s)? *How are you?*
cómodo a *comfortable, convenient*
el/la compañero/a mf *companion, classmate*
la compañía f *company*
comparar v *to compare*
compartir v *to share, divide*
competente a *competent*
completo a *complete/full*
comportarse vr *to behave*
el comportamiento m *behaviour*
comprar v *to buy*
las compras fpl *shopping*
comprender v *to understand*
comprensivo a *understanding*
con prep *with*
con permiso interj *excuse me*
el concierto m *concert*
concurrido a *busy, crowded*
el concurso m *competition*
las condiciones de trabajo fpl *working conditions*
conducir v *to drive, lead*
la conducta f *behaviour*
el/la conductor/a mf *driver, motorist*
conectar v *to connect*
el conejo m *rabbit*
la confianza f *confidence/trust*
confiar v *to trust*
la confitería f *sweet shop*
el conflicto m *conflict*
conocer v *to know, meet*

conseguir v *to achieve, manage, get*
el consejo m *advice*
conservar v *to maintain/ keep*
la consigna f *left-luggage office*
la construcción f *construction*
construir v *to build*
el/la consumidor/a mf *consumer*
consumir v *to use/ consume*
el/la contable mf *accountant*
contactar v *to contact*
la contaminación f *pollution*
contaminar v *to pollute*
contar v *to count, tell*
el contenedor m *container*
contento a *happy/ pleased*
contestar v *to reply, answer*
continuar v *to continue*
contra prep *against*
la contraseña f *password*
el contrato m *contract*
contribuir v *to contribute*
la conversación f *conversation*
conversar v *to talk/chat*
la copa f *cup, trophy, wine glass*
el corazón m *heart*
la corbata f *tie*
correcto a *correct*
corregir v *to correct*
correr el riesgo v *to run the risk*
el correo m *post*
el correo basura m *junk mail*
el correo electrónico m *email*
Correos m *post office*
correr v *to run*
la correspondencia f *post/ correspondence*
la corrida (de toros) f *bullfight*
cortar v *to cut*
cortés a *polite*
la cortina f *curtain*
corto a *short*
la cosa f *thing*
la costa f *coast*
costar v *to cost*
la costumbre f *custom*
creativo a *creative*
creer v *to think, believe*
crema a *cream (colour)*
la crema solar f *suntan lotion*
el crep m *pancake*
el cristal m *glass, crystal*
el cruce m *junction (road)*
cruzar v *to cross*
el cuaderno m *exercise book*
cuadrado a *square*
¿Cuál(es)? pron *Which/ What?*
la cualidad f *quality*
cuando ad *when*
¿Cuándo? ad *When?*
¿Cuánto/a? a/ad *How much?*
¿Cuánto cuesta(n)? *How much does it/ do they cost?*
¿Cuánto es? *How much is it?*
¿Cuánto vale(n)? *How much does it/ do they cost?*
¿Cuántos/as? a *How many?*
¿Cuántos años tiene(s)? *How old are you?*
cuarto a *fourth*
el cuarto m *room, quarter*
el cuarto de baño m *bathroom*
Cuba f *Cuba*
cubano a *Cuban*
cubrir v *to cover*
la cuchara f *spoon*
el cuchillo m *knife*
el cuello m *neck*
la cuenta f *bill, sum, account*
el cuero m *leather*
el cuerpo m *body*
¡Cuidado! interj *Careful!*
cuidadoso a *careful*
cuidar v *to look after, take care of*
la culpa f *fault/blame*
la cultura f *culture*
el cumpleaños m *birthday*
cumplir años v *to have a birthday*
el curso m *course*

D

dado que conj *give that/ since*
dañar v *to harm, damage, spoil*
el daño m *harm, damage*
dañoso a *damaging*
dar v *to give*
dar a v *to look onto*
dar de comer v *to feed*
dar igual v *to not matter*
dar las gracias v *to thank*
dar una vuelta v *to go for a walk/drive*
darse prisa vr *to hurry*
de prep *of, from*
de...a prep *from...to*
de acción a *action*
de aventura a *adventure*
de cerdo a *pork*
de cordero a *lamb*
¿De dónde? ad *Where from?*
de lujo a *luxury*
de manera que conj *so that*
de momento ad *at the moment*
De nada interj *You're welcome*
de nuevo ad *again*
de primero *for the first course*
¿De qué color? *What colour?*
¿De quién? pron *Whose?*
de repente ad *suddenly*
de ternera a *veal*
de vaca a *beef*
deber v *to owe, must, should*
los deberes mpl *homework*
debido a conj *due to*
débil a *weak*
decepcionado a *disappointed*
decepcionante a *disappointing*
decepcionar v *to disappoint*
decidir v *to decide*
décimo a *tenth*
decir v *to say*
dedicarse a vr *to devote oneself to*
el dedo m *finger*
el defecto m *defect/fault*
dejar v *to leave, allow*
dejar castigado v *to put in detention*
dejar de (hacer) v *to stop (doing)*
delante (de) prep *in front (of)*
delgado a *thin, slim*
delicioso a *delicious*
los/las demás mfpl *the others*
demasiado ad *too, too much*
el/la dentista mf *dentist*
dentro (de) ad/prep *inside*
dentro de... (horas) ad *in... (hours)*
el/la dependiente/a mf *shop assistant*
el deporte m *sport*
los deportes acuáticos mpl *watersports*
los deportes de invierno mpl *winter sports*
deportista a *sporty*
deportivo a *sports*
la depresión f *depression*
a la derecha ad *on the right*
(todo) derecho ad *straight ahead*
los derechos mpl *rights*
desafortunadamente ad *unfortunately*
desagradable a *unpleasant*
desaparecer v *to disappear*
el desastre m *disaster*
desayunar v *to have breakfast*
el desayuno m *breakfast*
descansar v *to rest*
el descanso m *rest, break*
descargar v *to download*
desconectar v *to disconnect*
describir v *to describe*
la descripción f *description*
descubrir v *to discover*
el descuento m *discount*
desde prep *from*
desde hace prep *since/ for*
desear v *to wish, desire*
el desempleo m *unemployment*
la desforestación f *deforestation*
desobediente a *disobedient*
el despacho m *office*
despacio ad *slowly*
despejado a *clear*
el desperdicio m *waste*
despertarse vr *to wake up*
después (de) ad *after, later on*
el destino m *fate/destiny*
la destrucción f *destruction*
destruir v *to destroy*
el desván m *loft*
la desventaja f *disadvantage*
el detalle m *detail, small gift*
detener(se) v(r) *to delay/ stop*
detestar v *to detest, hate*
detrás (de) ad/prep *behind*
devolver v *to give back, return*
el día m *day*
el Día de Reyes m *epiphany/6th January*
el día festivo m *bank holiday*
el día laborable m *working day*
diariamente ad *daily*
dibujar v *to draw*
el dibujo m *drawing, art*
los dibujos animados mpl *cartoons*
el diccionario m *dictionary*
diciembre m *December*
el diente m *tooth*
la dieta f *diet*
la diferencia f *difference*
diferente a *different*
difícil a *difficult*
la dificultad f *difficulty*
¡Dígame! interj *Hello (when answering the telephone)*
Dinamarca f *Denmark*
el dinero m *money*
el dinero de bolsillo m *pocket money*
la dirección f *direction/ address/management*
directo a *straight, direct*
el/la director/a mf *director, head*
el disco (compacto) m *disk/CD*
el disco duro m *hard disk*
la discoteca f *disco/ nightclub*
la discriminación f *discrimination*
disculpar(se) v(r) *to forgive/apologise*
la discusión f *argument*
discutir v *to argue, discuss*
diseñar v *to design*
el diseño m *design*
disfrutar v *to enjoy*
disponible a *available*
la distancia f *distance*
distinto/a (de) a *different (from)*
la diversión f *fun/hobby*
divertido a *fun, funny, amusing*
divertirse vr *to enjoy oneself*
divorciado a *divorced*
divorciarse vr *to get divorced*
el DNI = documento nacional de identidad m *ID card*
el divorcio m *divorce*
doblar v *to turn, to fold*
el doble m *double*
la docena f *dozen*
la documentación f *papers/ documents*
el documental m *documentary*
el documento m *document*
el dólar m *dollar*
doler v *to hurt*
el dolor m *pain, ache*
el domicilio m *home, residence*
el domingo m *Sunday*
¿Dónde? ad *Where?*
¿Dónde está? *Where is it?*
dormir(se) v(r) *to (go to) sleep*
el dormitorio m *bedroom*
Dr(a). = doctor(a) mf *doctor*
la droga (dura/blanda) f *(hard/soft) drug*
el/la drogadicto/a mf *drug addict*
drogarse vr *to take drugs*
la droguería f *chemist's/ drugstore*
la ducha f *shower*
ducharse vr *to have a shower*
dudar v *to doubt*
dulce a/ad *sweet, soft, gentle*
durante prep *during*
durar v *to last*
duro a *hard*

E

echar de menos v *to miss*
echar la culpa v *to blame*
ecológico a *environmentally-friendly*
económico a *economic, cheap*
la edad f *age*
el edificio m *building*

a educación física f *PE*
educar v *to educate*
educativo a *educational*
EEUU = Estados Unidos mpl *USA*
el efecto invernadero m *the greenhouse effect*
egoísta a *selfish*
el/la ejecutivo/a mf *executive*
el ejemplo m *example*
el ejercicio (físico) m *(physical) exercise*
el ejército m *army*
la electricidad f *electricity*
el/la electricista mf *electrician*
eléctrico a *electric, electrical*
los electrodomésticos mpl *electrical appliances*
elegante a *stylish*
elegir v *to choose*
emborracharse vr *to get drunk*
emigrar v *emigrate*
las emisiones fpl *emissions*
emocionante a *moving, exciting*
empezar v *to begin*
el/la empleado/a mf *employee*
el empleo m *employment, work, job*
la empresa f *company*
en prep *in, on*
en/por todas partes ad *everywhere*
en efectivo a/ad *in cash*
en este/ese momento ad *at the moment/at that time*
en las afueras ad *on the outskirts*
en paro a *unemployed*
en punto ad *on the dot*
en seguida ad *immediately*
en vez de ad *instead of*
enamorarse (de) vr *to fall in love (with)*
encantado a *delighted*
encantador a *delightful*
encantar v *to delight*
el/la encargado/a mf *manager*
encargado de a *in charge of*
encargarse vr *to deal with*
encender v *to light, turn on, ignite*
encima (de) ad/prep *on, above, over*
encontrar v *to find*
encontrarse vr *to meet/be situated*
encontrarse bien/mal vr *to feel well/ill*
la encuesta f *survey*
el/la enemigo/a mf *enemy*
la energía f *energy*
enérgico a *energetic*
enero m *January*
enfadarse vr *to get angry*
la enfermedad f *illness*
el/la enfermero/a mf *nurse*
enfermo a *ill*
enfrente (de) ad/prep *opposite, in front (of)*
¡Enhorabuena! interj *Congratulations!*
la ensalada f *salad*
enseñar v *to teach, show*
la enseñanza f *education, teaching*
ensuciar v *to dirty, get dirty*
entender v *understand*
entonces ad *then, after*
la entrada f *entry, entrance, ticket*
entrar v *to enter*
entre prep *between, among*
entregar v *to deliver, hand over*
el entrenamiento m *training*
entrenarse vr *to train*
entretenido a *entertaining*
la entrevista f *interview*
el entusiasmo m *enthusiasm*
entusiasta a *enthusiastic*
el envase m *container*
enviar v *to send*
el equipaje m *luggage*
el equipo m *team*
la equitación f *horse riding*
equivocado a *mistaken*
el error m *mistake*
es decir conj *that is (to say)*
la escalera f *stairs, ladder*
escocés a *Scottish*
Escocia f *Scotland*
escoger v *to choose*
escribir v *to write*
el/la escritor/a mf *writer*
escuchar v *to listen (to), hear*
la escuela f *school*
ese a *that*
el esfuerzo m *effort*
el espacio m *space*
los espaguetis mpl *spaghetti*
la espalda f *back*
España f *Spain*
español a *Spanish*
el español m *Spanish (language/ school subject)*
especial a *special*
la especialidad f *speciality*
el espectáculo m *show, performance*
el espejo m *mirror*
esperar v *to hope, expect, wait*
espléndido a *splendid*
el/la esposo/a mf *husband, wife*
el esquí m *skiing*
esquiar v *to ski*
la esquina f *corner*
esta noche ad *tonight*
estable a *stable*
la estación f *station*
la estación (del año) f *season*
la estación de autobuses f *bus station*
la estación de metro f *metro station*
la estación de servicio f *service station*
la estación de trenes f *train station*
el estadio m *stadium*
el estado m *state (marital)*
los Estados Unidos mpl *the USA*
el estanco m *tobacco/ cigarette shop*
el estante m *shelf*
la estantería f *bookcase*
estar v *to be*
estar a x kilómetros de v *to be x kilometres away from*
estar a x minutos de v *to be x minutes away from*
estar a favor v *to be in favour*
estar de acuerdo v *to agree*
estar de moda v *to be in fashion*
estar de vacaciones v *to be on holiday*
estar en contra v *to be against*
estar en forma v *to be in shape*
estar en huelga v *to be on strike*
estar en paro v *to be unemployed*
estar equivocado v *to be mistaken*
estar estresado v *to be stressed*
estar harto/a de v *to be fed up of*
estar situado/a v *to be located*
la estatua f *statue*
este/esta a *this*
éste/ésta/esto pron *this*
el este m *the East*
el estéreo m *stereo*
estimado a *dear (to start formal letters)*
el estómago m *stomach*
estrecho a *narrow*
la estrella f *star*
el estrés m *stress*
estresante a *stressful*
estricto a *strict*
estropear v *to spoil/ damage/break*
el estuche m *case (for glasses etc.)*
el/la estudiante mf *student*
estudiar v *to study*
los estudios mpl *studies*
estupendo a *wonderful*
estúpido a *stupid*
el euro m *euro*
Europa f *Europe*
europeo a *European*
evitar v *to avoid*
exactamente ad *exactly*
exacto a *exact*
el examen m *exam*
excelente a *excellent*
el éxito m *success*
la expectativa f *hope, prospect*
la experiencia laboral f *work experience*
la explicación f *explanation*
explicar v *to explain*
el exterior m *the outside*
la extinción f *extinction*
extranjero a *foreign*
el extranjero m *abroad*
el/la extranjero/a mf *foreigner*
extraordinario a *extraordinary*
extrovertido a *outgoing*

F

la fábrica f *factory*
fabuloso a *fabulous*
fácil a *easy*
la falda f *skirt*
falso a *false, fake*
la falta f *error*
faltar v *to lack, be missing, need*
la familia f *family*
la familia adoptiva f *adoptive family*
famoso a *famous*
el/la famoso/a mf *celebrity*
fantástico a *fantastic*
el/la farmaceútico/a mf *pharmacist*
la farmacia f *chemist's*
fascinante a *fascinating*
fascinar v *to fascinate*
fastidiar v *to annoy*
fatal a *awful*
favorable a *favorable*
favorito a *favourite*
febrero m *February*
la fecha f *date*
la fecha de nacimiento f *date of birth*
¡Felices Pascuas! *Happy Easter!*
¡Felices vacaciones! *Happy holidays!*
la felicidad f *happiness*
¡Felicidades! interj *congratulations!*
¡Felicitaciones! interj *congratulations!*
feliz a *happy*
¡Feliz año nuevo! *Happy New Year!*
¡Feliz cumpleaños! *Happy Birthday!*
¡Feliz santo! *Happy Saint's Day!*
femenino a *feminine*
fenomenal a *great*
feo a *ugly*
el ferrocarril m *railway*
festejar v *to celebrate*
la ficha f *file, counter, token*
la fiebre f *fever, temperature*
la fiesta f *party, holiday, festival*
la fiesta de cumpleaños f *birthday party*
el filete m *fillet/steak*
la filosofía f *philosophy*
el fin de semana m *weekend*
al final ad *in the end*
finalmente ad *finally*
firmar v *to sign*
la física f *physics*
físico a *physical*
flaco a *thin*
el flamenco m *flamenco*
el flan m *crème caramel*
la flauta f *flute*
la flor f *flower*
el folleto m *brochure*
en el/al fondo (de) ad/prep *in/at the back*
el/la fontanero/a mf *plumber*
el footing m *jogging*
la forma f *shape, way, method, form*
formal a *polite*
formar parte v *to be part*
la foto f *photo*
fracasar v *to fail*
el fracaso m *failure*
la frambuesa f *raspberry*
francés a *French*
el/la francés/esa mf *Frenchman/woman*
Francia f *France*
frecuente a *frequent*
el fregadero m *sink*
fregar los platos v *to wash up*
la fresa f *strawberry*
fresco a *fresh, cool*
el frigorífico m *refrigerator*
el frío m *cold*
frito a *fried*
la fruta f *fruit*
la frutería f *fruit shop, greengrocer's*
el fuego m *fire*
fuera (de) ad/prep *outside (of)*
fuerte a *strong*
la fuerza f *strength, force*
el/la fumador/a mf *smoker*
el/la fumador/a pasivo/a mf *passive smoker*
fumar v *to smoke*
la función f *function*
funcionar v *to function*
el fútbol m *football*
futuro a *future*
el futuro m *future*

G

las gafas fpl *(eye)glasses*
las gafas de sol fpl *sunglasses*
la galería (de arte) f *(art) gallery*

Gales m *Wales*
el/la galés/esa mf *Welshman/woman*
Galicia f *Galicia*
la galleta f *biscuit*
las gambas fpl *prawns*
el/la gamberro/a mf *hooligan*
ganar v *to earn, win*
el garaje m *garage*
la garganta f *throat*
los gases de escape mpl *exhaust*
la gasolina f *petrol*
la gasolina sin plomo f *unleaded petrol*
gastar v *to spend (money), wear away*
el/la gato/a mf *cat*
el gazpacho m *cold tomato soup*
el/la gemelo/a mf *twin*
la generación f *generation*
generalmente ad *generally*
el género m *gender*
generoso a *generous*
genial a *brilliant, great*
la gente f *people*
la geografía f *geography*
el gerente m *manager*
la gimnasia f *gymnastics, P.E.*
el gimnasio m *gymnasium, gym*
girar v *to turn*
global a *global*
glotón a *greedy*
el gobierno m *government*
el gol m *goal*
golpear v *to hit*
la goma f *glue, rubber*
gordo a *fat*
la gorra f *cap*
grabar v *to record*
gracias interj *thank you*
gracioso a *funny*
el grado m *degree, grade*
el gramo m *gramme*
Gran Bretaña f *Great Britain*
Gran Hermano m *Big Brother*
grande a *big, great*
los grandes almacenes mpl *department store*
la granja f *farm*
el/la granjero/a mf *farmer*
la grasa f *fat, grease*
gratis a/ad *free, for nothing*
gratuito a *free*
grave a *serious*
Grecia f *Greece*
la gripe f *flu*
gris a *grey*
grueso a *thick, stout, fat*
el grupo m *group*
los guantes mpl *gloves*
guapo a *beautiful, handsome*
guardar v *to save*
el/la guía mf *guide*
la guía (turística) f *guidebook*
el guión bajo m *underscore*
los guisantes mpl *peas*
la guitarra f *guitar*
gustar v *to like*

H

haber v *to have...*
la habitación f *room, bedroom*
la habitactión doble f *double room*
la habitación individual f *single room*
el/la habitante mf *resident*
el hábito m *habit*
hablador a *talkative, chatty*
hablando interj *speaking (answering the telephone)*
hablar v *to talk, speak*
hace (dos semanas) que v *for (two weeks)*
hacer v *to do, make*
hacer aerobic v *to do aerobics*
hacer cola v *to line up*
hacer daño v *to damage*
hacer ejercicio v *to do exercise*
hacer falta v *to need, lack*
hacer frío v *to be cold (weather)*
hacer la(s) compra(s) v *to do the shopping*
hacer prácticas v *to practise, train*
hacer transbordo v *to change*
hacer un aprendizaje v *to do an apprenticeship*
hacerse vr *to become*
hacia prep *towards, about*
la hamburguesa f *burger*
la hamburguesería f *burger stand*
hasta prep *until, up to*
hasta el (lunes) prep *until (Monday)*
hasta luego interj *see you later*
hasta mañana interj *see you tomorrow*
hasta pronto interj *see you soon*
hay v *there is, there are*
hay que v *it is necessary to*
el helado m *ice-cream*
la heladería f *ice-cream parlour*
helar v *to freeze*
el/la hermano/a mf *brother/sister*
el/la hermanastro/a mf *stepbrother/sister*
hermoso a *beautiful*
hervido a *boiled*
el hielo m *ice*
el hígado m *liver*
el/la hijo/a mf *son/daughter*
el/la hijo/a único/a mf *only child*
el hipermercado m *hypermarket*
la historia f *story, history*
histórico a *historical*
el hockey m *hockey*
el hogar m *home, hearth*
¡Hola! interj *Hello!*
Holanda f *Holland*
el/la holandés/esa mf *Dutchman/woman*
el hombre m *man*
el hombre de negocios m *businessman*
el hombro m *shoulder*
honesto a *honest*
honrado a *honourable, honest*
la hora f *hour*
el horario m *timetable*
el horario de trabajo m *working hours*
las horas de trabajo flexibles fpl *flexible working hours*
el horno m *oven*
horrible a *horrible/awful*
horroroso a *dreadful, horrible*
hoy ad *today*
el/la huérfano/a mf *orphan*
el huevo m *egg*
húmedo a *damp*
el humo m *smoke*

I

ideal a *ideal*
la identidad f *identity*
el idioma m *language*
la iglesia f *church*
igual que a *equal to, just like*
la igualdad f *equality*
la igualdad de derechos f *equal rights*
impaciente a *impatient*
el impermeable m *raincoat*
importante a *important*
imposible a *impossible*
impresionante a *impressive*
imprimir v *to print*
el incendio m *fire*
incluido a *included*
incluir v *to include*
incluso ad *even*
increíble a *incredible*
la independencia f *independence*
independiente a *independent*
la industria f *industry*
industrial a *industrial*
la influencia f *influence*
la información f *information*
informar(se) v(r) *to inform (oneself)*
la informática f *computing, IT*
el/la ingeniero/a mf *engineer*
Inglaterra f *England*
el inglés m *English (language)*
el/la inglés/esa mf *Englishman/woman*
injusto a *unjust, unfair*
inmediatamente ad *immediately*
el/la inmigrante mf *immigrant*
inmigrar v *immigrate*
inmóvil a *immobile, unmoving*
inquietante a *worrying*
inquietar(se) v(r) *to worry*
inseguro a *insecure*
la insolación f *sunstroke*
insolente a *rude*
las instalaciones fpl *facilities*
el instituto m *secondary school, college*
el instrumento m *instrument*
insultar v *to insult*
inteligente a *intelligent*
la intención f *intention*
intentar v *to try*
el intercambio m *exchange*
interesante a *interesting*
interesarse en vr *to be interested in*
el interior m *interior*
el internauta m *internet user*
el internet m *internet*
el/la intérprete mf *interpreter*
intimidar v *intimidate*
introvertido a *introverted*
la inundación f *flood*
inútil a *useless*
el invierno m *winter*
la invitación f *invitation*
el/la invitado/a mf *guest*
invitar v *to invite*
la inyección f *injection*
inyectar(se) v(r) *to inject (oneself)*
el iPod® m *iPod®*
ir v *to go*
ir a + infinitive v *to be going to (Future Tense)*
ir al extranjero v *to go abroad*
ir de compras v *to go shopping*
ir de vacaciones v *to go on holiday*
Irlanda f *Ireland*
irlandés a *Irish*
irse vr *to leave*
la isla f *island*
las Islas Canarias fpl *Canary Islands*
Italia f *Italy*
italiano a *Italian*
el IVA (impuesto sobre el valor añadido) m *VAT*
(a) la izquierda f *(on) the left*

J

jamás ad *never*
el jamón (de york) m *ham (boiled ham)*
el jamón serrano m *cured ham*
el Januká m *Hanukkah*
el jardín m *garden*
el/la jardinero/a mf *gardener*
el jazz m *jazz*
el/la jefe/a mf *boss, head, manager*
el jersey m *jumper*
joven a *young*
el/la joven mf *young man/woman*
la joyería f *jewellery, jeweller's shop*
jubilado a *retired*
jubilarse vr *to retire*
las judías verdes fpl *green beans*
el juego m *game, play*
el juego de ordenador m *computer game*
los Juegos Olímpicos mpl *Olympic Games*
el jueves m *Thursday*
el/la jugador/a mf *player*
jugar v *to play*
el jugo m *juice*
el juguete m *toy*
la juguetería f *toy shop*
julio m *July*
junio m *June*
juntos ad *together*
justificar v *to justify*
justo ad *just, exactly*
la juventud f *youth*

K

el kilo m *kilogramme*
el kilómetro m *kilometre*

L

laboral a *industrial*
el laboratorio m *laboratory*
al lado de prep *next door, at the side of*
el lado m *side*
el ladrón m *thief*
el lago m *lake*
la lámpara f *lamp*
la lana f *wool*
los lápices de colores mpl *colouring pencils*
el lápiz m *pencil*
largo a *long*
la lata f *tin, can*
latinoamericano a *Latin American*
el lavabo m *washbasin, washroom*
la lavadora f *washing machine*
el lavaplatos m *dishwasher*
lavar v *to wash*
lavar los platos v *to wash the dishes*
la lección f *lesson*
la leche f *milk*
la lechuga f *lettuce*
la lectura f *reading*
leer v *to read*
las legumbres fpl *vegetables, pulses*

lejos (de) ad/prep *far, far away (from)*
la lengua f *language, tongue*
lento a *slow*
la letra f *letter*
levantar la mano v *to put up one's hand*
levantarse vr *to get up*
la libertad f *freedom*
la libra (esterlina) f *pound (sterling)*
libre a *free, available*
la librería f *bookshop, bookcase*
el libro m *book*
la licenciatura f *university degree*
el limón m *lemon*
la limonada f *lemonade*
limpiar v *to clean*
limpio a *clean*
la línea f *line*
liso a *smooth, straight*
la lista f *list*
la lista de precios f *price list*
la literatura f *literature*
el litro m *litre*
la llamada f *call*
llamar por teléfono v *to call, phone*
llamarse vr *to be called*
la llave f *key*
la llegada f *arrival*
llegar v *to arrive*
llegar a ser v *to become*
lleno a *full*
llevar v *to wear, carry, take*
llevar puesto v *to wear*
llevarse bien/mal con vr *to get on well/badly with*
llorar v *to cry*
llover v *to rain*
la lluvia f *rain*
la lluvia ácida f *acid rain*
lo siento *I'm sorry*
loco a *mad*
lograr v *to achieve*
Londres m *London*
los (lunes) *on (Mondays)*
la lotería f *lottery*
luego ad *then, after*
el lugar m *place*
el lunes m *Monday*
la luz f *light/electricity*

M

la madera f *wood, timber*
la madrastra f *stepmother*
la madre f *mother*
la madre soltera f *single mother*
la madrugada f *early morning*
magnífico a *brilliant*
mal ad *badly, ill*
mal educado a *impolite, rude*
la maleta f *suitcase*
malgastar v *waste*
malo a *bad, wrong, ill, naughty*
maltratar v *to mistreat*
el maltrato m *ill-treatment*
la mamá f *mum, mummy*
mandar v *to send/order/be in charge*
la mano f *hand*
la manta f *blanket*
el mantel m *tablecloth*
mantenerse en forma vr *to keep fit*
la mantequilla f *butter*
la manzana f *apple, block of houses*
mañana ad *tomorrow*
la mañana f *morning*
el mapa m *map*
el maquillaje m *make-up*
la máquina f *machine*
la máquina de fotos f *camera*
el mar m *sea*
marcar (un gol) v *to score (a goal)*
la marea negra f *oil slick*
el marido m *husband*
los mariscos mpl *seafood*
marrón a *brown*
el martes m *Tuesday*
marzo m *March*
más (que) ad *more (than)*
la mascota f *pet*
masculino a *masculine*
matar v *to kill*
las matemáticas fpl *maths*
el matrimonio m *marriage*
mayo m *May*
mayor a *older*
la mayoría f *the majority*
el/la mecánico/a mf *mechanic*
la medalla f *medal*
la media hora f *half an hour*
la media pensión f *half board*
mediano a *medium, average*
la medianoche f *midnight*
las medias fpl *tights, stockings*
el/la médico/a mf *doctor*
la medida f *measure, measurement*
medio a *half*
en el medio a *in the middle*
el medio ambiente m *environment*
medioambiental a *environmental*
el mediodía m *midday*
medir v *to measure*
el Mediterráneo m *the Mediterranean*
mejor a *better, best*
mejorar v *to improve*
mejorarse vr *to get better*
la melena f *long hair*
el melocotón m *peach*
menor a *younger, youngest, smaller*
menos (que) ad *less (than)*
menos cuarto (time) a *quarter to*
el mensaje m *message*
mentir v *to lie*
la mentira f *lie*
mentiroso a *untruthful, lying*
el menú del día m *menu of the day*
el menú turístico m *tourist menu*
el mercado m *market*
la merienda f *teatime snack*
la merluza f *hake*
la mermelada f *jam*
el mes m *month*
la mesa f *table*
el metro m *metre, underground train*
mexicano a *Mexican*
México m *Mexico*
la mezquita f *mosque*
el microondas m *microwave*
la miel f *honey*
el/la miembro mf *member*
mientras (que) conj *while, meanwhile*
mientras tanto conj *meanwhile*
el miércoles m *Wednesday*
el militar m *soldier*
mínimo a *minimum*
el minuto m *minute*
mirar v *to look at, look, watch*
mismo a *same*
la mitad f *half*
mixto a *mixed*
la mochila f *backpack, rucksack*
la moda f *fashion*
el/la modelo mf *model*
moderno a *modern*
mojarse vr *to get wet*
molestar v *to trouble, disturb*
el momento m *moment*
la moneda f *coin*
el monedero m *purse*
el/la monitor/a *instructor, coach*
el monopatín m *skateboard*
el monopatinaje m *skateboarding*
la montaña f *mountain*
montañoso a *mountainous*
montar v *to ride, put together*
montar a caballo v *to ride a horse*
el monumento m *monument*
la moqueta f *fitted carpet*
morado a *purple*
morir v *to die*
mostrar v *to show*
la moto(cicleta) f *motorbike*
el motor m *engine, motor*
el (teléfono) móvil m *mobile phone*
el/la muchacho/a mf *boy/girl*
mucho a *a lot, many*
mucho gusto interj *it's nice to meet you*
mucho tiempo m *a long time*
mudarse de casa vr *to move house*
los muebles mpl *furniture*
muerto a *dead*
la mujer f *woman, wife*
la mujer de negocios f *businesswoman*
mundial a *worldwide*
el mundo m *world*
la muñeca f *doll, wrist*
el museo m *museum*
el/la músico/a mf *musician*
muy ad *very*

N

nacer v *to be born*
nacido a *born*
el nacimiento m *birth*
la nacionalidad f *nationality*
nada pron *nothing, not at all*
nada más pron *nothing more*
nadar v *to swim*
nadie pron *nobody*
naranja a *orange*
la naranja f *orange*
la naranjada f *orangeade*
la nariz f *nose*
la nata f *cream*
la natación f *swimming*
la naturaleza f *nature*
navegar v *to surf*
Navidad f *Christmas*
necesario a *necessary*
la necesidad f *necessity*
necesitar v *to need*
negativo a *negative*
negro a *black*
nervioso a *nervous*
nevar v *to snow*
la nevera f *refrigerator*
ni...ni conj *neither...nor*
la niebla f *fog*
el/la nieto/a mf *grandson/daughter*
la nieve f *snow*
ningún a *none/not any*
el/la niño/a mf *boy, girl*
el nivel m *level*
no ad *no, not*
no fumador m *non smoker*
la noche f *night*
Nochebuena f *Christmas Eve*
Nochevieja f *New Year's Eve*
el nombre m *name*
el noreste m *northeast*
normal a *normal*
normalmente ad *normally*
el noroeste m *northwest*
el norte m *north*
norteamericano a *North American*
Noruega f *Norway*
la nota f *note, mark, grade*
las noticias fpl *news*
la novela f *novel*
noveno a *ninth*
noviembre m *November*
el/la novio/a mf *fiancé(e), boy/girlfriend*
la nube f *cloud*
nublado a *cloudy, overcast (sky)*
nuboso a *cloudy*
nuevo a *new*
la nuez f *walnut*
el número m *number*
nunca ad *never*

O

o/u conj *or*
el objetivo m *aim*
obligatorio a *compulsory*
la obra benéfica f *charity work*
la obra de teatro f *play*
el/la obrero/a mf *workman/woman*
obtener v *to obtain*
el ocio m *leisure*
octavo a *eighth*
octubre m *October*
ocupado a *occupied, engaged*
ocuparse de vr *to look after*
ocurrir v *to happen, occur*
odiar v *to hate*
el oeste m *west*
ofender v *to offend*
ofenderse vr *to take offence*
la oferta f *offer*
la oficina f *office*
la oficina de cambio f *bureau de change*
la oficina de turismo f *tourist office*
el oído m *ear (inside part)*
oír v *to hear, to listen*
¡Ojo! interj *Look out!*
el ojo m *eye*
¡Olé! interj *Hooray!*
oler v *to smell*
el olor m *smell*
olvidar v *to forget*
la ONG f (Organización No Gubernamental) *NGO (Non-governmental Organisation)*
la opción f *option*
opinar v *to think, give your opinion*
la oportunidad f *opportunity*
optar v *to choose*
optativo a *optional*
optimista a *optimist*
el ordenador m *computer*
el ordenador portátil m *laptop*
la oreja f *ear (outer)*
organizar v *to organise*
orgulloso a *proud*
el oro m *gold*

oscuro a *dark*
el otoño m *Autumn*
otro a *another*
otra vez a *again*
el oxígeno f *oxygen*

P

paciente a *patient*
el padrastro m *stepfather*
el padre m *father*
los padres pl *parents*
la paella f *paella (rice dish)*
la paga f *pay, wages, pocket money*
pagar v *to pay*
pagar bien/mal v *to pay well/badly*
la página f *page*
la página web f *web page*
el país m *country*
el paisaje m *landscape*
el País Vasco m *Basque Country*
el pájaro m *bird*
la palabra f *word*
el palacio m *palace*
pálido a *pale*
el pan m *bread*
la panadería f *bakery*
el/la panadero/a mf *baker*
el panecillo m *bread roll*
la pantalla f *screen*
el pantalón m *trousers*
el pantalón corto m *shorts*
el panty m *tights*
el papá m *daddy*
Papá Noel m *Father Christmas*
el papel m *paper*
el papel higiénico m *toilet paper*
la papelera f *wastepaper basket/bin*
la papelería f *stationer's, stationery*
el paquete m *packet, parcel*
el par m *pair, couple*
para prep *for, in order to, so that*
¿Para/Por cuánto tiempo? *How long for?*
la parada f *stop*
parado a *stopped, still, unemployed*
el parador m *(state-run) hotel*
el paraguas m *umbrella*
parar v *to stop*
parecer v *to seem, appear, look like*
parecerse a vr *to look like*
parecido a *similar*
la pared f *wall*
la pareja f *couple, partner*
los parientes mpl *relatives*
el parking m *car park*
el paro m *unemployment, stoppage*
el parque m *park*
el parque de atracciones m *funfair*
el parque infantil m *playground*
el parque temático m *theme park*
el parque zoológico m *zoo*
la participación f *participation*
participar v *to participate*
el partido m *match/game, party (political)*
pasado a *past, last*
el pasado m *the past*
pasado de moda a *out of fashion/unfashionable*
pasado mañana ad *the day after tomorrow*
el/la pasajero/a mf *passenger*
el pasaporte m *passport*
pasar v *to pass, spend (time), happen*
pasar (la) lista v *to take the register*
pasar (por) v *to go past, through*
pasar la aspiradora v *to vacuum*
pasarlo bien/mal v *to have a good/bad time*
el pasatiempo m *hobby, pastime*
pasear (el perro, etc.) v *to take (the dog, etc.) for a walk*
pasearse vr *to go for a walk/stroll*
el paseo m *walk, stroll*
el pasillo m *corridor*
el paso m *step, way*
(dar un) paso v *(to take) a step*
el paso subterráneo m *subway*
la pasta f *pasta, paste*
el pastel m *cake, pie*
la pastelería f *baker's, cake shop*
la patata f *potato*
las patatas fritas fpl *chips, crisps*
el paté m *paté*
el patinaje m *skating*
patinar v *to skate*
el patio m *courtyard*
las pecas fpl *freckles*
el pedazo m *piece*
pedir v *to order, ask for*
pedir permiso v *to ask permission*
peinarse vr *to comb your hair*
la pelea f *quarrel, fight*
pelear(se) v(r) *to quarrel/fight*
la película f *film*
el peligro m *danger*
peligroso a *dangerous*
pelirrojo a *red-haired*
el pelo m *hair*
la pelota f *ball*
la peluquería f *hairdresser's*
el/la peluquero/a mf *hairdresser*
los pendientes mpl *earrings*
pensar v *to think*
la pensión f *guest house*
la pensión completa f *full board*
el pepino m *cucumber*
peor a *worse, worst*
pequeño a *small, little*
la pera f *pear*
perder v *to lose*
la pérdida de tiempo f *waste of time*
perdón interj *sorry! pardon me*
perdonar v *to forgive*
perdone interj *sorry! forgive me*
perezoso a *lazy*
perfecto a *perfect*
la perfumería f *perfume shop*
el periódico m *newspaper*
el periodismo m *journalism*
el/la periodista mf *journalist*
el periquito m *parakeet*
permanente a *permanent*
el permiso m *licence, permit*
el permiso de conducir m *driving licence*
permitir v *to allow*
pero conj *but*
el perrito caliente m *hot dog*
el/la perro/a mf *dog*
las persianas fpl *(Venetian) blind*
la persona f *person*
el personaje m *celebrity, character*
la personalidad f *personality*
la perspectiva f *perspective*
Perú m *Peru*
peruano a *Peruvian*
pesado a *heavy*
pesar v *to weigh*
la pesca f *fishing*
la pescadería f *fishmonger's*
el pescado m *fish (dead, for eating)*
pescar v *to fish*
pesimista a *pesimistic*
el peso m *weight*
el petróleo m *oil, petroleum*
el pez m *fish*
el piano m *piano*
picante a *hot, spicy*
el pie m *foot*
la piel f *skin, leather*
la pierna f *leg*
la pila f *battery*
la pimienta f *pepper (spice)*
el pimiento m *pepper (vegetable)*
el ping-pong m *table tennis*
pintado a *painted*
el/la pintor/a mf *painter*
la pintura f *painting*
la piña f *pineapple*
la piscina f *swimming pool*
el piso m *flat, floor*
la pista f *court, track, piste*
la pista de hielo f *ice rink*
la pizarra f *blackboard*
el plan m *project*
planchar v *to iron*
el planeta m *planet*
el plano m *plan, map*
la planta m *floor, plant*
la planta baja f *ground floor*
el plástico m *plastic*
la plata f *silver*
el plátano m *banana*
el plato m *plate, dish, course*
el plato combinado m *one course set meal*
el plato del día m *dish of the day*
la playa f *beach*
la plaza f *square*
la plaza de toros f *bullring*
pobre a *poor*
la pobreza f *poverty*
poco a *little, few*
un poco a *a little*
poco sano a *unhealthy*
pocas veces ad *rarely*
poder v *to be able, can*
el policía m *policeman*
el policíaco m *detective, crime (film)*
el polideportivo m *sports centre*
el pollo m *chicken*
poner v *to put*
poner la mesa v *to lay the table*
ponerse vr *to become*
ponerse a vr *to begin to*
ponerse de acuerdo vr *to agree*
el pop m *pop music*
por prep *for, through, by, along*
por año ad *per year*
por anticipado ad *in advance*
¿Por dónde? ad *Where?*
por ejemplo conj *for example*
por eso ad *therefore*
por favor interj *please*
por fin ad *finally*
por lo general ad *in general*
por lo tanto ad *therefore*
¿Por qué? ad *Why?*
por supuesto ad *of course*
por un lado/por otro lado conj *on one hand/ on the other hand*
por una parte/por otra parte conj *on one hand/ on the other hand*
la porción f *portion*
porque conj *because*
portugués a *Portuguese*
el porvenir m *future*
la posibilidad f *possibility*
posible a *possible*
positivo a *positive*
la postal f *postcard*
el postre m *sweet, dessert*
practicar v *to practise*
las prácticas laborales fpl *work experience*
práctico a *practical*
el precio m *price*
preciso a *necessary, precise*
la preferencia f *priority, preference*
preferido a *favourite*
preferir v *to prefer*
la pregunta f *question*
preguntar v *to ask*
el prejuicio m *prejudice*
el premio m *prize*
la preocupación f *worry*
preocupado a *worried*
preocuparse vr *to worry*
preparar v *to prepare*
prescindir de v *to do without*
la presentación (oral) f *presentation*
presente a *present*
prestar v *to lend*
el presidente m *president*
primario a *primary/basic*
la primavera f *spring*
la primera clase f *first class*
primero a *first*
el/la primo/a mf *cousin*
el principio m *beginning*
privado a *private*
probar v *to try, test, prove, taste*
probarse vr *to try on*
el problema m *problem*
producir v *to produce*
los productos químicos mpl *chemicals*
el/la profesor/a mf *teacher*
profundo a *deep, profound*
el programa m *programme*
el/la programador/a mf *computer programmer*
prohibido a *prohibited*
prohibir v *to prohibit, ban*
prometer v *to promise*
el pronóstico m *forecast*
pronto ad *soon/early/ ready*
la propina f *tip*
propio a *own*
proteger v *to protect*
la provincia f *province*
próximo a *next*
prudente a *sensible*
la prueba f *proof, test*
publicar v *to publish*
la publicidad f *publicity, advertising*
el público m *public, audience*
el pueblo m *village, people*
el puente m *bridge*
la puerta f *door, gate*
el puerto m *port*
pues conj *well, then*
el puesto m *job/position*
los pulmones mpl *lungs*
el pulpo m *octopus*
el punto m *dot, point, spot, place*
puntocom m *dotcom*

nouns — **m**: masculine **f**: feminine **pl**: plural **v**: verb **vr**: reflexive verb **a**: adjective

Q

que conj *that, who, which*
¡Qué! ad *How!*
¿Qué? pron *What?, Which?*
¡Que aproveche! interj *Enjoy your meal!*
¡Qué asco! interj *How disgusting!*
¡Qué bien! interj *That's great!*
¿Qué día? *What day?*
¿Qué fecha? *What date?*
¿Qué hay? *How's it going?*
¿Qué hora es? *What time is it?*
¡Qué horror! interj *How awful!*
¡Qué lástima! interj *What a shame!*
¡Que lo pase(s) bien! interj *Have a good time!*
¿Qué pasa? *What's happening?*
¡Qué pena! interj *What a shame!*
¿Qué tal? *How's it going?*
¡Qué va! interj *As if!*
(el mes, etc) que viene ad *next (month, etc.)*
quedar v *to suit (clothing)*
quedar en v *to agree*
quedarse vr *to stay*
la queja f *complaint*
quejarse vr *to complain*
querer v *to want, love*
querer decir v *to mean*
el queso m *cheese*
¿Quién? pron *Who?, Whom?*
la química f *chemistry*
químico a *chemical*
quince días mpl *fortnight*
quinto a *fifth*
el quiosco m *kiosk, news stand*
quisiera v *I/he/she/you would like*
quizás ad *perhaps*

R

la ración f *portion*
el racismo m *racism*
racista a *racist*
el radiador m *radiator*
el Ramadán m *Ramadan*
el rap m *rap music*
rápido a *fast*
raramente ad *rarely*
raro a *strange*
rasgado a *ripped/torn*
el rato m *while, amount of time*
el ratón m *mouse*
la razón f *reason*
razonable a *reasonable*
la reacción f *reaction*
las rebajas fpl *sales*
la rebeca f *cardigan*
recargable a *rechargeable*
la recepción f *reception*
el/la recepcionista mf *receptionist*
recibir v *to receive*
el recibo m *receipt*
reciclable a *recyclable*
el reciclaje m *recycling*
reciclar v *to recycle*
recientemente ad *recently*
recoger v *to pick up, collect*
recomendar v *to recommend*
reconocer v *to recognise*
recordar v *to remember*
el recreo m *break, playtime*
el recuerdo m *souvenir, memory*
el recurso m *resource*
la red f *internet*
redondo a *round*
reducir v *to reduce/ shorten*
el reembolso m *reimbursement*
regalar v *to give (as a present)*
el regalo m *present, gift*
la región f *region*
la regla f *rule, ruler*
regresar v *to return*
el regreso m *return*
regular a *average*
la rehabilitación f *rehabilitation*
rehabilitar v *to rehabilitate*
reírse vr *to laugh*
relacionarse con vr *to be related to*
relajarse vr *to relax*
el relámpago m *flash of lightning*
la religión f *religion*
rellenar v *to fill up, stuff, fill in (form)*
el reloj m *watch, clock*
la Renfe f *Spanish rail network*
repartir v *to share, divide*
el reparto a domicilio m *delivery service*
repasar v *to revise*
repetir v *to repeat*
el reproductor de mp3 m *MP3 player*
la reserva f *reservation*
reservado a *reserved*
reservar v *to reserve*
resfriado a *suffering from a cold*
la residencia (para ancianos) f *care home (for the elderly)*
residencial a *residential*
los residuos orgánicos mpl *organic waste*
resolver v *to solve*
respetar v *to respect*
el respeto m *respect*
respirar v *to breathe*
respiratorio a *breathing*
responder v *to respond, reply, answer*
la responsabilidad f *responsibility*
responsable a *responsible*
la respuesta f *reply, answer*
el restaurante m *restaurant*
el resto m *the rest*
el resultado m *result*
el resumen m *summary*
el retraso m *delay*
la reunión f *meeting*
reutilizar v *to reuse*
la revista f *magazine*
rico a *rich, wealthy, delicious*
ridículo a *ridiculous*
el riesgo m *risk*
riguroso a *severe, harsh, tough*
el río m *river*
la Rioja f *Rioja*
rizado a *curly*
robar v *to rob, steal*
el robo m *theft, robbery*
el rock m *rock music*
la rodilla f *knee*
rojo a *red*
romántico a *romantic*
romper v *to break*
la ropa f *clothes*
rosa a *pink*
rosado a *pink*
rubio a *blonde, fair-haired*
la rueda f *wheel*
el ruido m *noise*
ruidoso a *noisy*
Rusia f *Russia*

S

el sábado m *Saturday*
saber v *to know/taste*
sabroso a *tasty*
el sacapuntas m *pencil sharpener*
sacar v *to take out, get*
sacar buenas/malas notas v *to get good/bad marks*
sacar fotos v *to take photos*
el saco de dormir m *sleeping bag*
la sal f *salt*
la sala de chat f *chat room*
la sala de espera f *waiting room*
la sala de estar f *living room*
la sala de fiestas f *night club*
la sala de profesores f *staff room*
salado a *salty, amusing*
el salario m *salary, wage*
la salchicha f *sausage*
el salchichón m *Spanish sausage*
la salida f *departure, exit*
salir (de) v *to go out (of/from), leave, depart*
el salón m *lounge, living room*
el salón de actos m *assembly room*
la salsa f *sauce*
la salud f *health*
saludable a *healthy*
saludar v *to greet*
saludos mpl *greetings, best wishes*
salvar v *to save*
las sandalias fpl *sandals*
la sangre f *blood*
la sangría f *sangria (drink)*
sano a *healthy*
el santo m *saint's day*
la sardina f *sardine*
el satélite m *satellite*
la sección f *section*
seco a *dry*
el/la secretario/a mf *secretary*
secundario a *secondary*
la sed f *thirst*
la seda f *silk*
seguir v *to follow, continue*
según prep *according to*
el segundo m *second*
segundo a *second*
seguro a *safe, certain, sure*
seguro de sí mismo a *self-assured*
la selección f *selection*
seleccionar v *to choose*
el sello m *stamp*
la selva f *jungle, rainforest*
el semáforo m *traffic lights*
la semana f *week*
la Semana Santa f *Easter*
sencillo a *simple, single*
el senderismo m *hiking*
la sensación f *feeling*
sensible a *sensitive*
sentarse vr *to sit down*
el sentido de humor m *sense of humour*
el sentimiento m *feeling*
sentir(se) v(r) *to feel*
la señal f *sign*
el/la señor/a mf *man/woman, Mr/Mrs, sir/madam*
la señorita f *miss, young lady*
separado a *separate*
separar la basura v *to separate the rubbish*
separarse vr *to separate/ break up*
se(p)tiembre m *September*
séptimo a *seventh*
la sequía f *drought*
ser v *to be*
ser aficionado/a de v *to be a fan of*
la serie f *series, serial*
serio a *serious*
seropositivo a *HIV positive*
el servicio m *service*
los servicios mpl *the toilets*
la servilleta f *serviette/ napkin*
servir v *to serve*
la sesión f *session/ performance*
severo a *harsh/strict*
sexista a *sexist*
sexto a *sixth*
si conj *if*
sí ad *yes*
sí pron *himself, herself, itself*
el sida m *AIDS*
siempre ad *always*
la sierra f *mountain range*
el siglo m *century*
siguiente a *next, following*
el silencio m *silence*
la silla f *chair*
el sillón m *easy chair, armchair*
similar a *similar*
simpático a *nice, friendly*
sin prep *without*
sin duda ad *undoubtedly*
sin embargo ad *however*
los "sin techo" mpl *the homeless*
sincero a *honest*
el síndrome de absistencia m *withdrawal symptoms*
sino conj *but (rather)*
el síntoma m *symptom*
el sitio m *place, space, room*
el sitio web m *website*
situado a *situated*
el sobre m *envelope*
sobre prep *on, about, around (time)*
sobresaliente a *outstanding*
el/la sobrino/a m *nephew/ niece*
la sociedad f *society*
el/la socio/a mf *member*
¡Socorro! interj *Help!*
el sofá m *sofa*
el sol m *sun*
solamente/sólo ad *only, just*
el/la soldado mf *soldier*
solicitar v *to apply*
la solicitud f *application*
solo a *alone*
soltero a *single, unmarried*
la solución f *solution*
la sombra f *shadow, shade*
el sombrero m *hat*
la sombrilla f *parasol*
el sonido m *sound*
sonreír(se) v(r) *to smile*
la sopa f *soup*
sorprendido a *surprised*
el sótano m *basement*
el spray m *aerosol*
el squash m *squash*
Sr (Señor) *Mr*
Sra (Señora) *Mrs*
Srta (Señorita) *Miss, Ms*
Sta (santa) *saint*
subir v *to go up, rise*
sucio a *dirty*
la sudadera f *sweatshirt*

sudamericano a South American
Suecia f *Sweden*
el sueldo m *salary, wage, pay*
el suelo m *floor*
el sueño m *dream*
el suéter m *sweater*
suficiente a *enough*
sugerir v *to suggest*
Suiza f *Switzerland*
el supermercado m *supermarket*
supervisar v *to supervise*
el suplemento m *supplement*
el sur m *south*
el sureste m *southeast*
el suroeste m *southwest*
el surtido m *selection, range*
suspender v *to fail*
la sustancia química f *chemical*

T

la tabacalera f *tobacconist's, stationer's*
el tabaco m *tobacco*
el tabaquismo m *nicotine poisoning*
tal vez *perhaps*
el Talgo m *inter-city express train*
la talla f *size (clothes)*
el tamaño m *size*
también ad *also*
tampoco ad *neither*
tan...como ad *as...as*
tanto...como ad *as...as*
las tapas fpl *snacks*
la taquilla f *box office, ticket office*
tardar v *to take time*
tarde ad *late*
la tarde f *afternoon, evening*
la tarea f *task*
las tareas fpl *homework*
la tarjeta f *card*
la tarjeta de crédito f *credit card*
el tarro m *jar, pot*
la tarta f *cake, tart*
el taxi m *taxi*
el/la taxista mf *taxi driver*
la taza f *cup*
el té m *tea*
el teatro m *theatre*
el tebeo m *comic*
el teclado m *keyboard*
el/la técnico/a mf *technician*
la tecnología f *technology*
el tejado m *roof*
la tela f *cloth, material*
el teléfono m *telephone*
el teléfono móvil m *mobile phone*
la telenovela f *soap opera*
el teletrabajo m *telemarketing*
la tele(visión) f *TV*
el televisor m *television set*
el tema m *theme, subject*
el temperamento m *temperament*
la temperatura f *temperature*
templado a *mild, temperate*
temprano ad *early*
el tenedor m *fork*
tener v *to have*
tener (15) años v *to be (15) years old*
tener calor v *to be hot*
tener dolor de v *to have pain in/hurt*
tener ganas v *to feel like*
tener hambre v *to be hungry*
tener lugar v *to take place*
tener miedo v *to be afraid*
tener prisa v *to be in a hurry*
tener que v *to have to*
tener razón v *to be right*
tener sed v *to be thirsty*
tener sueño v *to be sleepy*
tener suerte v *to be lucky*
el tenis m *tennis*
el tenis de mesa m *table tennis*
la tentación f *temptation*
tercero a *third*
terminar v *to finish*
la terraza f *terrace*
el/la testigo/a mf *witness*
el texto m *text*
tibio a *cool, tepid*
el tiempo m *time, weather*
el tiempo libre m *free time*
la tienda f *shop, tent*
la tienda con fines benéficos f *charity shop*
la tienda de comestibles f *grocery shop*
la tienda de ropa f *clothes shop*
la Tierra f *Earth*
las tijeras fpl *scissors*
tímido a *shy, timid*
el tío m *uncle*
típico/a a *typical*
el tipo m *type, kind*
el tipo de cambio m *exchange rate*
tirar v *to throw, throw away, pull*
tirarse vr *to throw oneself*
el título m *university degree*
tocar v *to play (instrument)/touch*
todas las (semanas) a *every (week)*
todavía ad *yet, still*
todo a *all, every*
todo recto ad *straight on*
todos a *every*
tolerante a *tolerant*
tomar v *to take, have*
tomar el sol v *to sunbathe*
tomar un año libre/sabático v *to take a year out*
el tomate m *tomato*
tonto a *silly, stupid*
torcer v *to turn, twist*
el torero m *bullfighter*
la tormenta f *storm*
tormentoso a *stormy*
el torneo m *tournament, competition*
el toro m *bull*
torpe a *slow, clumsy*
la tortilla f *omelette*
la tortuga f *tortoise*
la tos f *cough*
la tostada f *slice of toast*
tóxico a *toxic*
trabajador a *hardworking*
el/la trabajador/a mf *worker*
trabajar v *to work*
el trabajo m *work, job*
los trabajos manuales mpl *manual labour*
la tradición f *tradition*
tradicional a *traditional*
traducir v *to translate*
el/la traductor/a mf *translator*
traer v *to bring*
el tráfico m *traffic*
Tráigame... *Bring me...*
el traje m *suit*
tranquilo a *calm, quiet*
transportar v *to transport*
el transporte m *transport*
el transporte público m *public transport*
el tranvía m *tram, local train*
tratar v *to try, treat, deal with*
tratarse de vr *to be about*
travieso a *naughty*
el tren m *train*
el trimestre m *term*
triste a *sad*
la trompeta f *trumpet*
el trozo m *piece, bit*
el trueno m *thunder*
el túnel m *tunnel*
el turismo m *tourism*
el/la turista mf *tourist*
turquesa a *turquoise*
el turrón m *Spanish nougat*
el/la tutor/a mf *tutor*

U

la UE f (Unión Europea) *EU*
últimamente ad *recently*
último a *last, latest, final*
único a *only, unique*
el uniforme m *uniform*
la universidad f *university*
unos a *some*
unos (diez) a *about (ten)*
usar v *to use*
el/la usario/a mf *user*
el uso m *use, function*
útil a *useful*
utilizar v *to use*
las uvas fpl *grapes*

V

las vacaciones fpl *holidays*
vacío a *empty*
vago a *vague, lazy*
la vainilla f *vanilla*
vale interj *OK, fine*
valer la pena v *to be worthwhile*
valiente a *brave*
el vandalismo m *vandalism*
los vaqueros mpl *jeans*
varios a *several*
el vaso m *glass (drinking)*
(tres) veces fpl *(three) times*
el/la vecino/a mf *neighbour*
el/la vegetariano/a mf *vegetarian*
el vehículo m *vehicle*
la vela f *candle, sailing*
la vena f *vein*
el/la vendedor/a mf *vendor, seller*
vender v *to sell*
venir v *to come*
la venta f *sale*
la ventaja f *advantage*
la ventana f *window*
ver v *to see, watch*
el verano m *summer*
la verdad f *truth*
verdadero a *true*
verde a *green*
la(s) verdura(s) f(pl) *vegetables*
el vestíbulo m *hall, foyer*
vestido a *dressed*
el vestido m *dress*
vestirse vr *to get dressed*
el vestuario m *clothes, wardrobe, dressing room*
el/la veterinario/a mf *vet, veterinary*
la vez f *time, occasion*
la vía f *way, lane (motorway), track*
viajar v *to travel*
el viaje m *journey*
el/la viajero/a mf *traveller*
la víctima f *victim*
la vida f *life*
la videoclub f *videoshop*
el videojuego m *video game*
el vidrio m *glass (material)*
viejo a *old*
el/la viejo/a mf *old man/woman*
el viento m *wind*
el viernes m *Friday*
el vinagre m *vinegar*
el vino (blanco/rosado/tinto) m *wine (white/rosé/tinto)*
la violencia f *violence*
violento a *violent*
violeto a *violet*
el violín m *violin*
el violoncelo m *cello*
la visita f *visit*
el/la visitante mf *visitor*
visitar v *to visit*
el/la viudo/a mf *widower/widow*
la vivienda f *home, dwelling*
vivir v *to live*
vivo a *alive, lively*
el vocabulario m *vocabulary*
volar v *to fly*
el voleibol m *volleyball*
voluntario a *voluntary*
el/la voluntario/a mf *volunteer*
volver v *to return, turn*
volver a + inf v *to do again*
volverse vr *to turn round, to turn back*
vomitar v *to vomit, be sick*
la voz f *voice*
el vuelo m *flight*

W

el wáter m *toilet*
el windsurf m *windsurfing*

Y

y/e conj *and*
y cuarto a *quarter past*
y media a *half past, and a half*
ya ad *already, yet, now*
ya (que) conj *since, as*
el yogur m *yoghurt*

Z

la zanahoria f *carrot*
la zapatería f *shoe shop*
las zapatillas de deporte fpl *trainers*
los zapatos mpl *shoes*
la zona f *zone, area*
la zona peatonal f *pedestrian precinct*
el zoo m *zoo*
el zumo m *juice*

Index

Index